Contents

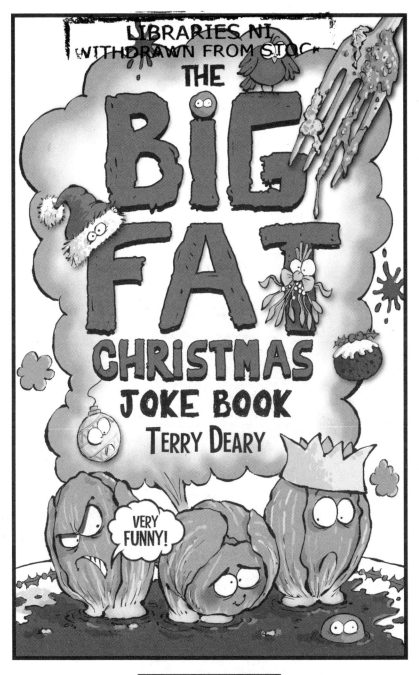

THE BIG FAT CHRISTMAS JOKE BOOK

Terry Deary

VERY FUNNY!

SCHOLASTIC

Scholastic Children's Books,
Euston House, 24 Eversholt Street,
London NW1 1DB, UK

A division of Scholastic Ltd
London ~ New York ~ Toronto ~ Sydney ~ Auckland
Mexico City ~ New Delhi ~ Hong Kong

First published in the UK by Scholastic Ltd, 2000
This edition published 2019

Father Christmas Joke Book
First published in the UK by Scholastic Publications Ltd, 1990
Text copyright © Terry Deary, 1990
Illustrations copyright © Stuart Trotter, 1990

The Great Father Christmas Robbery
First published in the UK by Scholastic Publications Ltd, 1991
Text copyright © Terry Deary, 1991
Illustrations copyright © Stuart Trotter, 1991

Cover illustration by Mike Phillips
© Scholastic Ltd, 2019

ISBN 978 1407 19648 0

Printed and bound by CPI Group (UK) Ltd, Croydon, CR0 4YY

www.scholastic.co.uk

Introduction

Me name is Father Christmas,
Some call me Santa Claus,
I'm here to bring you joy, my friends,
At Christmas time, because
. . . it's me job.

I live up at the North Pole
With all me little gnomes.
They can be pests, but stay with me
'Cos they've no other homes
. . . to go to.

We spend the lovely summer days
Just making lots of toys.
Then Christmas Eve we dash around
And give them to all boys
. . . and girls.

But winter nights we sit around
A roaring, great log fire.
We then tell jokes and stories
Till our eyes and voices tire
. . . and we go to bed.

A happy time we have then,
With jokes from all the gnomes,
But best of all they like to hear
The Father Christmas poems
. . . like this one.

One winter night Gnome Gnancy
Cried, "Hey, Father Christmas, look!
It's time we all sat down and wrote
These jokes up in a book
. . . for kids."

"A great idea that!" I agreed.
"Ho-ho! Ho-ho! Ho-ho!
I'll put in all me funny poems."
The gnomes all shouted "No!"
. . . but I have anyway.

So here's a book of Monster Laughs
And fun for Christmas time.
(I'd say "For all the family"
But can't think of a rhyme
. . . to go with family.)

So all the best at Christmas
Peace and goodwill to all.
And don't forget the mince pies
And the sherry when I call
. . . at your house to deliver all your presents.

ON THE FIRST DAY OF CHRISTMAS
MY TRUE LOVE SENT TO ME

ONE CHRISTMAS JOKE BOOK

Hello!
I'm a gnome and me name is Gnancy. Gnancy The Gnome.
I'm one of Father Christmas' helpers. There are seven of us who help him pack the presents and deliver them every Christmas.
First of all there's Gnorman The Gnome . . .

I wouldn't say Gnorman was small, but he used to be a lumberjack on a mushroom farm!

GNORMAN

GNANCY

10

In fact, he's so small that he has to stand on a ladder to fasten his shoe laces!

Then there's Gnora The Gnome . . .

I wouldn't say Gnora was ugly, but if beauty's skin deep then she was born inside out!

I wouldn't say Gnora was cross-eyed, but when she cries the tears run down her back!

She'd make a terrible teacher – she has no control of her pupils!

Of course you must know Gnigel The Gnome. He's not too bright is Gnigel.

TEACHER: Gnigel! Give me a sentence with the word gnome in it!

GNIGEL: Er . . . the man's house burnt down so . . . he hadn't a gnome to go to!

GNORA

GNIGEL

Then there's Gnellie. She's always poorly . . .

GNELLIE: Doctor, doctor! I keep seeing pink and green spots in front of my eyes!

DOCTOR: Good gracious! Have you seen an optician?

GNELLIE: No . . . just pink and green spots!

DOCTOR: I mean, have you ever had your eyes checked?

GNELLIE: No. They've always been blue!

Or Gneil. You wouldn't be too keen on him! He's so mean!

FATHER CHRISTMAS: How do I stop Gneil being airsick on the sledge?

GNANCY: Put a five pound note between his teeth and stick his head over the side of the sledge.

GNELLIE

GNEIL

And you must have met Gnocker! He's always on the wrong side of the front door . . .

Gnock! Gnock!
Who's there?
You.
You who?
Yoo-hoo! Nice to see you!

GNOCKER

Father Christmas is a jolly old chap. We have lots of happy jokes around Christmas time. You can always tell we're having a good time from the noise we make . . .

What goes "Ho! Ho! Ho! Thump!"?
Father Christmas laughing his head off!

We live at the North Pole, of course. Very cold, the North Pole.

"It's so cold outside," Gnora The Gnome said, "that I just watched a polar bear jump from one iceberg to another and it froze in mid-air!"

"That's impossible," Father Christmas said. "The law of gravity won't allow that!"

"Oh, I know," Gnora said, "but the law of gravity's frozen too!"

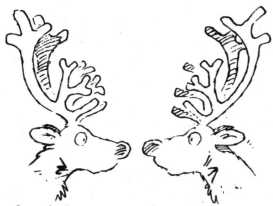

Only the reindeer can stand the cold . . .

"Father Christmas has two reindeer," Gnora the Gnome said. "He calls one Edward and the other one Edward! I bet you can't tell me why he does that!"

"Oh, yes I can," Gnorman the Gnome said. "Because two 'Eds are better than one, of course!"

And as the reindeer say before they tell you jokes . . .

These jokes will sleigh you!

So, be warned!!! Reading The Father Christmas Joke Book *can damage your brain cells . . . if you have any. And laughing can split your side – but if that happens just go for a fast run . . . you're sure to get a stitch in it!*

ON THE SECOND DAY OF CHRISTMAS
MY TRUE LOVE SENT TO ME

TWO CHRISTMAS CAROLS

Everybody has their favourite song at Christmas.
What's yours? Here at the North Pole we have a
favourite . . .

What song do Father Christmas' gnomes sing to him when he comes home cold on Christmas night?
Freeze a jolly good fellow!

But it's not just at the North Pole where they like their Christmas songs. In Africa they have them too . . .

GNORA:	What's Tarzan's favourite Christmas song?
GNORMAN:	Jungle bells, of course.
GNELLIE:	But what about his chimp?
GNEIL:	King Kong merrily on high, of course!

Not to mention the Sahara desert . . .

GNANCY:	So, what's the top of the desert pops at Christmas?
GNIGEL:	No-well, No-well!
GNORMAN:	The three wise men crossed the desert, didn't they? What did they sing?
GNEIL:	They sang, "Oh camel ye faithful!"
GNELLIE:	But what did the camels sing?
GNORA:	"All things bright and beautiful, All creatures grunt and smell!"

GNANCY:	They didn't have camels. They had cars and sang, "We three kings of Orient are Driving off in our old cars; One's a Ford and one's a Mini, And one is a Jaguar."
GNORA:	Rubbish! What they really sang was . . . "We three Kings of Orient are Trying to smoke a rubber cigar, It was loaded with explosive . . . BANG!! Now we're with yonder stars!"
GNORMAN:	So what did the shepherds sing, smarty pants?
GNORA:	Everybody knows that!

"While shepherds washed their
socks by night
All seated by the tub
An angel of the Lord flew down
And gave them all a scrub!"

Of course Gnocker had to stick his oar in . . .

Gnock, Gnock!
Who's there?
Our Wayne!
Our Wayne who?
Our Wayne in a manger!

*But Gnocker The Gnome isn't so amused when
people come knocking on **his** door at midnight.*

Gnock, Gnock!
Who's there?
Carol singers!
Carol singers! Do you know what flaming time of night it is?
No. But if you hum it we'll sing it!

So do you know the favourite Christmas song of these people?

What's a hairdresser's favourite Christmas song?
"Oh comb all ye faithful"

A football supporter?
"Yule never walk alone"

Bugs Bunny?
"Lettuce with a gladsome mind"

A talkative princess in a tower?
"Silent knight!"

Mind you, not everybody enjoys Christmas. Fairies sing this sad ditty at Christmas time . . .

A fairy has a hard time,
Up where the tinsel flickers;
A wand of gold stuck in her hand,
A fir tree up her knickers!

And it isn't just fairies who have a bad time at Christmas . . .

Oh little town 'neath moonlit skies
How still we see thee sleep.
As through the streets and on the roofs
A hooded figure creeps.
He climbs down all your chimneys
He carries a large sack . . .
He fills it with your valuables
Then quickly hurries back!

Now Gnora The Gnome is an awful singer . . . but, alas, that doesn't stop her trying.

One night Gnora went carol singing. She knocked on the door of a house and began to sing. A man with a violin in his hand came to the door. Within half a minute tears were streaming down his face! Gnora went on singing for half an hour, every carol she knew – and some she didn't. At last she stopped.

"I understand," she said softly. "You are remembering your happy childhood Christmas days. You're a sentimentalist!"

"No," he snivelled. "I'm a musician!"

But what is Father Christmas' favourite carol?

Father Christmas used to like "I'm dreaming of a quiet Christmas", but since we got a television at the North Pole he has a new favourite . . .
"Jingle Bells,
Batman smells,
Robin flew away.
The Batmobile has lost its wheels
Now it's a bat-mo-sleigh!"

THREE CHRISTMAS KNOCKERS

Did you know that Father Christmas' gnomes are afraid of Christmas?

GNIGEL: What do Gnomes fear most about Christmas?

GNOCKER: They're afraid Father Christmas will give them the sack!

Seriously, though, Father Christmas looks after us really well. It's not a lot of fun being a gnome. Especially if you're tiny like Gnorman.

GNORMAN: When I went to school I was hopeless at sport. In fact I once got lapped in the long jump! Everyone else was captain of the cricket or captain of the netball, captain of the rugby, captain of the football or captain of the swimming team. Teacher made me captain of the embroidery team!

And we all had a hard time finding a job . . .

GNIGEL: Before Father Christmas gave me a job I was offered work as a clown in a flea circus.

GNORA: Before Father Christmas gave me a job I was a novelist – but I was fed up with being called a "short" story writer.

GNORMAN: Before Father Christmas gave me a job I was a judge – but I got fed up with crooks saying, "These little things are sent to try us"!

GNELLIE: Before Father Christmas gave me a job I used to work as a body guard – to a dolls' house.

Gneil used to claim he was small but super-strong . . .

GNEIL: I'm so strong I could lift a reindeer with one hand.

GNORA: Yeah, but where are we going to find a one-handed reindeer?

But we all have our pets to keep us company . . .

GNIGEL: I have a dwarf elephant for a pet.

GNORA: What do you call a dwarf elephant?

GNIGEL: Trunk-ated!

GNORMAN:	What's that thing on your shoulder, Gneil?
GNEIL:	That's not a thing it's a newt!
GNORMAN:	What do you call him?
GNEIL:	I call him Tiny.
GNORMAN:	Why do you call him Tiny?
GNEIL:	Because he's my-newt!
GNELLIE:	Gnancy, what's that on your head?
GNANCY:	A sausage.
GNELLIE:	Is it your pet?
GNANCY:	No.
GNELLIE:	Is it to make you look taller?
GNANCY:	No.
GNELLIE:	So what is it?
GNANCY:	Why don't you ask it?
GNELLIE:	Sausage? What are you doing on Gnancy's head?
SAUSAGE:	I'm a head banger, of course!
GNOCKER:	Have you seen Gnancy's sausage? It looks like a Father Christmas or a hot dog.
GNIGEL:	A Father Christmas or a hot dog! What's the difference between a Father Christmas and a hot dog?
GNOCKER:	One wears a red suit . . . the other just pants.

And that reminds me. Gnocker knows all the worst jokes in the North Pole! Here are some of the best . . . you wouldn't want to hear the worst!

Gnock, Gnock!
Who's there?
Police.
Police who?
Police let me in; it's freezing out here!
SLAM

Gnock! Gnock!
Who's there?
I'm just knocking to say your door-bell's broken!
I know – I want to be considered for a No-bel prize!

Gnock! Gnock!
Who's there?
Snow!
Snow White?
No. 'Snow place like home.
You fooled me there. SLAM!

Gnock! Gnock!
Who's there?
Icy!
Icy road?
No, I–cy you're still at home then.
Curses! I'm covered in silver paper!
Covered in silver paper?
Yes! I'm foiled again!

Gnock! Gnock!
Who's there?
Wooden shoe.
Wooden shoe who?
Wooden shoe like to know?
Not really! SLAM!

Gnock! Gnock!
Who's there?
Carol!
Christmas Carol?
No. Carol be parked in the garage.
They get worse. SLAM!

Gnock! Gnock!
Who's there?
Ken!
Ken who?
Ken I come in?
Not if you tell awful jokes like that!
You'll let me in sooner or later.
No I won't. SLAM!

Gnock! Gnock!
Who's there?
Wendy.
Don't tell me . . . "Wendy red, red robin comes bob, bob bobbin' along"?
You've heard it.
Heard it? I wrote it! SLAM!

Gnock! Gnock!
Who's there?
Cook!
Cook who?
A cuckoo? In December?
SLAM!

Gnock! Gnock!
Who's there?
The famous Memory man!
The famous Memory man who?
Er . . . what was the question again?
SLAM!

Gnock! Gnock!
Who's there?
Butcher!
Butcher with the turkey?
No. Butcher name down here. I've got a Christmas
present for you.
Oh! Do come in!
I told you!

Gnock! Gnock!
Who's there?
Ghost.
Well, don't spook till you're spooken to! SLAM!

*So, with a pest like Gnocker around you can see why
there's only* **one** *answer to a knock on the door.*

GNOCK!!
GNOCK!

GO AWAY!!

FOUR CHRISTMAS PRESENTS

Christmas is the time for giving presents. And it's our job to help Father Christmas fill the sacks, load the sleigh and fly around the world delivering them. Being gnomes, we can get down to the places Father Christmas can't reach. We also get to read the letters to Father Christmas. And some people do ask for funny presents.

But not everyone gets what they expect . . .

Dear Father Christmas,
I am nearly bald. This
Christmas could you please
send me something to keep
my hair in.
    Signed
        E.G. Hedd.

FATHER CHRISTMAS:	Send him a paper bag.
GNEIL:	Send him a comb; I'll bet he never parts with it!

People don't just write to us for presents. They ask their parents too . . .

LITTLE GIRL:	Mammy, mammy! Can I have a puppy for Christmas?
MOTHER:	Certainly not. You can have turkey like everybody else!
LITTLE BOY:	Dad! Can I have a broken drum for Christmas?
DAD:	The best thing you could have asked for. You can't beat it!

LITTLE BOY: Daddy, Daddy! Can I have a wombat for Christmas?

DAD: What would you do with a wombat?

LITTLE BOY: Play wom, of course, stupid!

Of course the shops can be very helpful at Christmas, even though they're so busy.

GNORMAN: I don't understand why we can't have Christmas in July, when the shops aren't so crowded!

Shop assistants often help husbands and wives choose presents for each other . . .

MAN: My wife would like an unusual watch.

ASSISTANT: Certainly, sir. This one has insects in place of numbers.

MAN: So how do you tell the time?

ASSISTANT: Easy. Look! It's just coming up to fly past flea.

WOMAN:	Have you something for my husband? He has flat feet.
ASSISTANT:	Why not buy him a foot pump?
WOMAN:	And he suffers from water on the knee.
ASSISTANT:	So buy him some drainpipe trousers!

MAN:	I want some silk handkerchiefs for my wife.
ASSISTANT:	Certainly, sir. What size nose does she have?
MAN:	Actually she wanted something with diamonds but I only have two pounds.
ASSISTANT:	So, buy her a pack of cards.

MAN:	That train set looks fantastic. I'll take one.
ASSISTANT:	I'm sure your son will love it, sir!
MAN:	(sighs) Oh, yes . . . I suppose he would. You'd better give me two, then.

WOMAN:	What would you give to the man who has everything?
ASSISTANT:	Penicillin?
WOMAN:	He'd really like a tie to match his eyes.

ASSISTANT:	Blue, brown, green or grey?
WOMAN:	You don't do "bloodshot" I suppose?

Children can sometimes be very tiresome to buy presents for . . .

WOMAN:	Excuse me, do you have a kitten for my little girl?
ASSISTANT:	Sorry, madam, we don't do swaps.
WOMAN:	I mean, have you got any kittens going cheap?
ASSISTANT:	Certainly not! They all go miaow!
WOMAN:	My son would like a snake.
ASSISTANT:	We have a lovely boa constrictor.
WOMAN:	He'd also like a Lego set.
ASSISTANT:	So buy him a boa constructor!

MAN: Do you have a pink car for my daughter?

ASSISTANT: Sorry, sir, we're all sold out. It seems everyone in the country has bought a pink car this week.

MAN: You realize what this means?

ASSISTANT: Yes, sir. We're slowly turning into a pink car-nation!

MAN: I'd like a magician's set for my son.

ASSISTANT: Is he a beginner?

MAN: No! He's been practising the sawing-people-in-half trick for years.

ASSISTANT: Is he an only child?

MAN: No, no! He has a lot of half-brothers and sisters.

Not everyone gets what they want for Christmas – or wants what they get . . . with millions of presents given every Christmas there are bound to be a few disappointments . . .

YOUNG MAN: Did you like the parrot I bought you darling? It sings, dances, tells jokes and recites poetry. What did you think of it?

GIRL: Well, to be honest, it was a bit tough, but the stuffing was nice.

WIFE:	Darling, you know that shock-proof, waterproof, anti-magnetic, un-breakable watch you bought me?
HUSBAND:	Yes, darling.
WIFE:	Well, it caught fire.
HUSBAND:	Good grief.
WIFE:	But it's all right. I threw it in the river to put it out.
HUSBAND:	It cost too much to throw away.
WIFE:	It's all right. I fished the watch out of the river and it's still running.
HUSBAND:	The watch is still running?
WIFE:	No. The river, stupid!

And even Scott of the Antarctic and Mrs Scott of the Antarctic had difficulty buying the right Christmas presents . . .

LITTLE BOY:	My Christmas stocking's got a hole in it.
FATHER:	Of course it has, dipstick. That's to get the presents in.
LITTLE BOY:	I asked for a hundred stocking fillers and all I got was this creepy crawly.
FATHER:	You *got* a hundred stocking fillers . . . that centipede has a hundred legs!
GIRL:	But I asked for a stereo radio. This isn't stereo.
MOTHER:	Yes it is. You just have to place your ears ten metres apart!

The real highlight of Christmas for us gnomes is Boxing Day when we get our own presents . . .

GNIGEL:	What did you get for Christmas, Gnancy?
GNANCY:	A mystery book.
GNIGEL:	What's it called?
GNANCY:	*The Case of the Stolen Chestnut* by Nick McConker.
GNELLIE:	I hear Ugly Gnora Gnome got a mud pack to make her more beautiful!

44

GNORMAN: She did.

GNELLIE: Did it work?

GNORMAN: It really improved her appearance for three days.

GNELLIE: Then what went wrong?

GNORMAN: The mud fell off.

GNELLIE: Gnora reckons she has the face of a sixteen-year-old girl!

GNORMAN: She had – but we made her give it back!

FIVE CHRISTMAS CRACKERS

When we have our Christmas dinner we pull our crackers, put on the paper hats ... and then we read the cracker jokes!

GNORA: Why did the chicken cross the football pitch?

GNELLIE: Because the referee whistled for a fowl!

GNORMAN: What drink do frogs like best?

GNANCY: Croaker-cola!

GNIGEL:	What do you get if you cross a kangaroo with an octopus, a sheep and a zebra?
GNOCKER:	A striped, woolly jumper with eight sleeves!

GNEIL:	Did you hear about the stupid plastic surgeon?
GNIGEL:	Yes. He stood in front of the fire and melted!

GNORMAN:	What time is it when you see an elephant sitting on your television?
GNORA:	Time to get a new television!

GNANCY:	Father Christmas lost his umbrella but he didn't get wet! Why not?
GNELLIE:	Because it wasn't raining!

GNIGEL:	Why can't a bike stand up by itself?
GNEIL:	Because it's two-tyred!

Some of the cracker jokes are very old . . .

I say, I say, I say! My wife's gone to the West Indies!
Jamaica?
No. She was quite happy to go!

GNELLIE: What do you get if you cross a whale with a bird that quacks?

GNANCY: Moby Duck!

GNORMAN: How do witches tell the time?

GNELLIE: With a witch-watch!

GNORMAN: What do you do if your dog has ticks?

GNORA: Don't wind him up!

GNEIL: How can you get your name in lights the world over?

GNIGEL: Change your name to Emergency Exit!

GNANCY: What do you get if you cross a gnome with a vampire?

GNORMAN: A monster that sucks the blood out of your kneecaps!

GNORMAN: Doctor, Doctor! Everyone thinks I'm a liar!

DOCTOR: I don't believe you!

GNOCKER: What flower can you eat?

GNELLIE: A cauli-flower!

Gnock! Gnock!
Who's there?
Dishes!
Dishes who?
Dishes Father Christmas, so let me in!

GNORA: What's the best way to catch a rabbit?

GNELLIE: Hide behind a bush and make a sound like a carrot!

GNANCY: How do you start a polar-bear race?

GNORMAN: Say "Ready! Teddy! Go!"

GNOCKER: Which animal should you *not* play cards with?

GNIGEL: A cheetah!

GNEIL: What do you get if you cross a hen with a bedside clock?

GNORA: An alarm cluck!

GNANCY: What would you do if a rhino charged you?

GNIGEL: Pay him!

GNOCKER: Why couldn't the sailors play cards?

GNORA: Because the captain was standing on the deck!

GNEIL: What do you get hanging from Father Christmas' roof?

GNIGEL: Tired arms!

GNORMAN:	I'm letting my pet pig sleep on my bed!
GNEIL:	What about the smell?
GNORMAN:	He'll just have to get used to it!
GNORA:	Who delivers presents to baby sharks at Christmas?
GNORMAN:	Santa Jaws.
GNORA:	Where are the Andes?
GNORMAN:	On the end of the armies!
GNELLIE:	What do you get if you cross a cowboy with an octopus?
GNANCY:	Billy the Squid.
GNORA:	Waiter! Water! My Christmas pudding is off!
WAITER:	Off? Where to?

GNEIL: Who wrote the book, *The Awful Comedown*?

GNIGEL: Lucy Lastick!

GNORMAN: If I'm standing at the North Pole, facing the South Pole, and the East is on my left hand, what's on my right hand?

GNIGEL: Fingers.

GNOCKER: How do monkeys make toast?

GNORMAN: Stick some bread under the gorilla!

GNOCKER: What did the police do when the hares escaped from the zoo?

GNEIL: They combed the area!

GNORMAN: Why was the turkey in the pop group?

GNELLIE: Because he was the only one with drum-sticks!

GNELLIE: How does Father Christmas climb up a chimney?

GNORA: He uses a ladder in the stocking!

GNORA: Why do you call your dog Metalworker?

GNIGEL: Because every time he hears a knock he makes a bolt for the door.

GNOCKER: What song did Cinderella sing as she waited four months for her photos to come back from the chemist?

GNIGEL: "Some Day My Prints Will Come!"

ON THE SIXTH DAY OF CHRISTMAS MY TRUE LOVE SENT TO ME

SIX PANTO TICKETS

The big Christmas treat for us gnomes is when Father Christmas takes us all to the theatre to see the pantomime. Of course, Father Christmas thinks he's too famous and popular to need tickets for the panto.

FATHER CHRISTMAS: (To box office girl) All right, my good lady, my face is my ticket.

BOX OFFICE ATTENDANT: Then you'd better watch out . . . there's a feller inside who has the job of punching the tickets!

Even the reindeer wanted to go to the panto –
so Father Christmas booked them into the
stalls.

Ghosts love to go to the theatre at Christmas –
they like to watch a good phantomime!

*Mind you, going to the theatre with Father
Christmas can be a bit embarrassing. He's forever
popping out to get an ice-cream – and he's far too fat
to squeeze back in.*

**FATHER
CHRISTMAS:** (To lady with a feathered hat)
Excuse me, but did I step on
your toes on my way out to get an
ice-cream?

LADY: You certainly did!

**FATHER
CHRISTMAS:** Oh good! That means I'm back
in the right row!

*And you see such funny characters at the panto-
mime . . .*

GNELLIE: Who's that little girl who wears a
red cape and goes round shouting
"Knickers" at the Big Bad Wolf?

**FATHER
CHRISTMAS:** That's Little Rude Riding Hood.

GNEIL:	I wouldn't let that Cinderella play on *my* hockey team.
FATHER CHRISTMAS:	Why not?
GNEIL:	'Cos she keeps running away from the ball!

The pantomime we went to see this year had all the usual characters. First there was the "Dame" . . . but she looked an awful lot like a man dressed up to me!

The pantomime dame was called old Mother Hubbard. She had her song, of course:

Old Mother Hubbard
Went to the cupboard
To get her poor doggy a bone.
When she got there
The cupboard was bare
So the dog bit her leg.

PRINCE HANSEL.

OLD MOTHER HUBBARD.　　GRETEL RED RIDING HOOD.　　BARON STONEY BROKE.　　HELMUT HARDKNUT.

Now old Mother Hubbard's daughter was called Gretel and she had this red hood for riding. So she was known as Gretel Red Riding Hood. One day Old Mother Hubbard sent Gretel Red Riding Hood on an errand . . .

I WANT YOU TO VISIT GRANNY IN HER FOREST COTTAGE. SHE'S ILL.

POOR GRAN! PERHAPS I SHOULD TAKE HER SOME GOOD, WHOLESOME FOOD!

FOOD! FOOD! WHERE WILL WE GET FOOD? YOUR OLD MOTHER HUBBARD WENT TO THE CUPBOARD TO GET THE POOR DOGGY A BONE, BUT WHEN SHE GOT THERE THE CUPBOARD WAS SO BARE EVEN THE MICE HAD MOVED OUT. OH GRETEL RED RIDING HOOD, IF ONLY YOUR FATHER, ROBIN HOOD WERE ALIVE.

AH, YES, I WISH I'D KNOWN HIM. I'VE HEARD SO MUCH ABOUT HIM. HE USED TO ROB THE RICH TO GIVE TO THE POOR, DIDN'T HE?

NOT EXACTLY. HE USED TO ROB THE RICH 'COS THE POOR HAD NOTHING WORTH PINCHING!

And off our heroine went to Granny's cottage. Then the villain arrived. There's always a villain in a pantomime. In this one it was evil Baron Stoneybroke and his nasty henchman, Helmut Hardknut.

59

61

But then handsome Prince Hansel came on the scene. He was in disguise of course. In fact he looked a lot like a woman, just as Old Mother Hubbard looked a lot like a man. Very confusing, pantomimes. Even more confusing was Gretel Red Riding Hood in the forest. With Helmut Hardknut disguised as a wolf to catch her the only help she had was from the talking trees . . . whoever heard of a talking tree? Gretel Red Riding Hood hadn't at first!

63

And the panto ended with Old Mother Hubbard marrying Baron Stoneybroke, with Prince Hansel marrying Gretel Red Riding Hood . . .

and with Helmut Hardknut being arrested . . .

And of course everyone lived HAPPILY EVER AFTER!

SEVEN GREEDY GNOMES

Of course Gneil wouldn't go to a pantomime in case someone asked him to buy an ice-cream.

GNIGEL: What's Gneil's favourite Christmas game?

GNORA: Mean-opoly, of course!

GNORMAN: Someone bought Gneil a clock for Christmas. He put it straight in the bank.

GNELLIE: Why did he do that?

GNORMAN: He was trying to save time!

GNOCKER: But he broke his clock, didn't he?

GNANCY: That's right. He punched it.

GNOCKER: Why did he do that?

GNANCY: He said it was self-defence. He said the clock struck first!

Mind you, Gneil doesn't like to be called "mean". He says it all started with his dad . . .

GNEIL: My dad was so mean he wouldn't let me have a sledge. He told me to slide down the hill on my little brother.

GNELLIE: And Gneil's dad was too mean to pay for his swimming lessons. He just took Gneil down to the river and threw him in. It didn't work. Gneil kept getting out of the sack.

But all of Gneil's family are like that . . .

Gneil's family have the tidiest weddings the North Pole has ever seen . . . that's because all the confetti is on elastic.

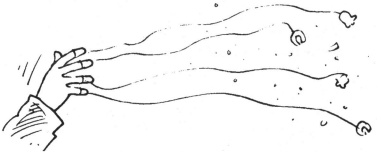

Some carol singers called at Gneil's house and said they were collecting for the local orphanage . . . so Gneil's mum gave them a couple of orphans!

Gneil's uncle was always burgling houses. He used to take a shower when he'd finished filling his sack with loot – so he could make a clean getaway!

He was once caught stealing a stop watch – but the judge gave him a second chance.

So that's why Gneil is the way he is.

Gneil's so mean that he has a lock on his dustbin.

Gneil's so mean that when he takes 10p out of his purse the Queen blinks in the light.

Gneil's so mean that he wakes up in the night to see if he's lost any sleep.

Gneil's so mean that when he left school he decided to be a baker . . . because he wanted to make lots of dough.

Gneil's so mean that he once found a pair of crutches and broke both of his legs so that he could use them!

Now there are lots of stories about Gneil's meanness. Like when he was at school . . .

TEACHER: Tell me, Gnellie, if I have 20p and ask Gneil for another 30p how much will I have?

GNELLIE: Please, miss, 20p!

TEACHER: Gnellie, you don't know your arithmetic.

GNELLIE: Please, miss, you don't know your Gneil!

Gneil bought the cheapest canoe he could get to paddle round the Arctic Sea. It was so cheap it had no heater. One day he was freezing cold so he broke off some of the wood at the front and started a little fire in the cockpit of his kayak. That warmed him up a bit so he broke off some more. Soon there was only half his kayak left . . . and the first wave that came along sank him. Father Christmas had to rescue him and gave him a good telling off.

"Let that be a lesson to you, Gneil!"

"I know, I know!" the poor gnome moaned. "Don't tell me! I can't half my kayak and heat it!"

One day Gneil went up to Father Christmas and said, "Tell me, Father Christmas, are you superstitious?"

"Not at all," Father Christmas replied.

"Good," Gneil said. "Then will you lend me £13 please?"

Gneil was always trying to borrow money, of course. But there was one time when he offered some . . .

One summer Father Christmas decided to go for a holiday in the Canary Islands. (He'd heard they were cheap!) He'd just finished packing the sledge when Gnellie told him that there was no snow in the Canary Islands. The sledge wouldn't go!

"What shall I do?" Father Christmas asked.

"Well," Gnellie replied, "my brother has a Porsche for sale . . ."

"I've got one on the front of my house," Father Christmas said.

"No, Father Christmas, I said a Porsche, not a porch . . . it's a car. Anyway, he's selling it for twenty thousand pounds – it's a bargain!" Gnellie explained.

So Father Christmas went to his piggy bank, broke it open and took out his money. "Oh, dear!" he moaned. "I've only got nineteen-thousand, nine-hundred and ninety-nine pounds and ninety pence! What shall I do?"

He dashed to the front door and saw Gneil walking down the road outside. "Gneil! Gneil!" Father Christmas cried. "Can you give me ten pence to buy a Porsche?"

Gneil's greedy little eyes lit up! "Certainly, Father Christmas!" he grinned. "Here's *twenty* pence – get me one too!"

ON THE EIGHTH DAY OF CHRISTMAS
MY TRUE LOVE SENT TO ME

EIGHT STUFFED TURKEYS

Christmas is a time for eating and drinking – even at the North Pole . . .

Father Christmas and the seven gnomes don't have a turkey for Christmas, they have an octopus . . . it doesn't taste half as nice, but at least everyone gets a leg!

To tell the truth, turkeys are a bit expensive. Father Christmas went to a butcher's and saw that the turkeys were 90p a pound. He said to the butcher, "Do you raise them yourself?"

"Of course I do," the butcher replied. "They were only 50p a pound this morning!"

Gnigel's mother bought a huge turkey. "That must have cost a fortune!" Gnigel cried. "Actually I got it for a poultry amount," she said.

We're usually too busy to cook our own Christmas dinner at that time of the year. We always end up eating at the "Greasy Penguin Cafe". There's a sign that says: "The Greasy Penguin – Eat Dirt Cheap" . . . but, as Gneil says, "Who wants to eat dirt?"

It's in The Good Food Guide to Christmas Breakfasts *by Egall Runney.*

It's also the only place in the North Pole where the dustbins have indigestion.

We always start with the soup . . .

FATHER CHRISTMAS:	Waiter! Waiter! There's a spider in my soup!
WAITER:	Sorry, sir, it's the fly's day off.
GNORMAN:	Waiter! Waiter! There's a caterpillar on my Christmas dinner.
WAITER:	That's all right, mate, caterpillars don't eat much!

GNELLIE: Waiter! Waiter! There's a fly in the butter!

WAITER: Yes, miss, it's a butter-fly.

GNORA: Waiter! Waiter! Why is this biscuit crying?

WAITER: Ah, miss, that's 'cos its mum's been a wafer too long.

GNANCY: Waiter! Waiter! Can you make a sandwich spread?

WAITER: Yeah! I'll just sit on it.

GNEIL: Waiter! Waiter! This soup's expensive.

WAITER: What do you expect? It's 24 carrot soup!

GNOCKER: Waiter! Waiter! These chicken legs have no knees!

WAITER: Yes that's because it's a cock chicken. You'd have to go to London for the knees.

GNOCKER: Why?

WAITER: Because all the cock-knees are in London.

GNORMAN: Waiter! Waiter! This turkey tastes like an old settee.

WAITER:	Well, you asked for something with plenty of stuffing.
GNORMAN:	But it's tough!
WAITER:	(Trying a piece) Tastes tender enough to me!
GNORMAN:	It should be! I've just chewed that bit for twenty minutes!
FATHER CHRISTMAS:	I wanted a whole turkey. This one only has one leg!
WAITER:	Perhaps it's been in a fight.
FATHER CHRISTMAS:	Well take it back and bring me the winner!

GNEIL:	Waiter! Waiter! This turkey's disgusting!
WAITER:	Well, you asked for a foul roast, didn't you?
GNANCY:	Waiter! Waiter! I'll bet even a turkey wouldn't drink the coffee here!
WAITER:	Of course not . . . it would go to a Nest-cafe.
GNORMAN:	This turkey's fit for nothing.
WAITER:	A tur-key's always good for something.
GNORMAN:	What?
WAITER:	Opening Turkish doors.
GNORA:	Waiter! Waiter! Bring me a crocodile sandwich and make it snappy!

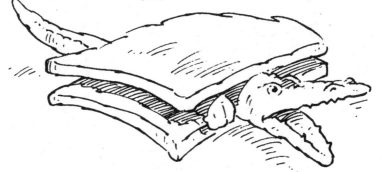

WAITER: And would you like some fast
vegetables with it?

GNORA: What are your fastest vegetables?

WAITER: Runner beans, of course.

GNOCKER: Waiter! Waiter! Bring me an omelette.

WAITER: Would you like a French or a
Spanish omelette?

GNOCKER: I don't mind . . . I want to eat it
not talk to it!

GNEIL: Waiter! Waiter! This lemon is
damaged.

WAITER: Don't worry, it just needs some
lemon-aid.

GNELLIE: Waiter! Waiter! Is that policeman
over there eating turkey?

WAITER: No, madam . . . he's eating
truncheon meat.

GNORMAN:	Waiter! Waiter! Is that Eskimo over there eating turkey?
WAITER:	No, sir. Eskimos eat whale meat and blubber.
GNORMAN:	Well if I ate whale meat I'd blubber.
GNORA:	But where do they get whale meat from?
WAITER:	The fish-mongers, madam. They buy it by the ton.
GNORA:	But how do they weigh a whale?
WAITER:	I expect they take it to the whale-weigh station.

GNORMAN:	Waiter! Waiter! This stuffing is odd. It's sausage meat at one end – but the other end is bread.
WAITER:	I know, sir. We're short of money at the moment. The manager's having trouble making both ends meat.

GNANCY:	Waiter! Waiter! I'd like Father Christmas stew.
WAITER:	Er . . . how do you make Father Christmas stew?
GNANCY:	You keep him waiting half an hour!

FATHER CHRISTMAS: Last year's Christmas pudding was so awful I threw it in the ocean.

WAITER: That's probably why the ocean's full of currants!

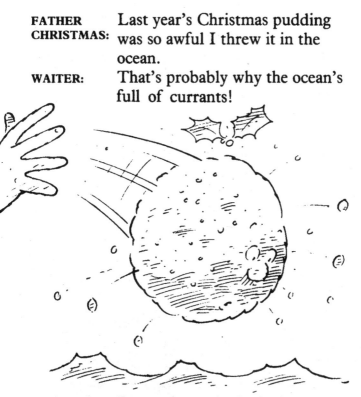

GNOCKER: But, waiter, what's the best way to keep a pudding?

WAITER: Don't eat it.

GNELLIE: Waiter! Waiter! Could you bring me some double cream for my pudding?

WAITER: No double cream, sorry. Will two singles do?

GNORMAN: Who made this Christmas pudding?

WAITER: Our chef. He's a little green man who lives in a toadstool.

GNORMAN: What did he use to make it?

WAITER: Elf-raising flour, of course.

GNIGEL: Waiter! Waiter! Have you ever tasted turkey soup?

WAITER: Turkey's soup? I've never met a turkey who could cook! The only turkeys we had here had terrible manners.

GNIGEL: They did?

WAITER: Yes, sir. They used to gobble at the table.

*If you want to see someone with **real** problems at Christmas, then look at a turkey . . .*

Did you hear about the stupid turkey?
It was looking forward to Christmas!

Why did the turkey cross the road?
To prove it wasn't chicken.

And why did the one-eyed turkey cross the road?
To get to the Bird's Eye shop.

What's a turkey's favourite television programme?
A duckumentary!

And three for afters . . .

How can you tell an owl's wiser than a chicken?
Well, did you ever hear of Kentucky Fried owl?

How do you tell the difference between tinned turkey and tinned custard?
Look at the labels!

What do you get if you pour boiling water down a rabbit hole?
Hot cross bunnies, of course.

ON THE NINTH DAY OF CHRISTMAS
MY TRUE LOVE SENT TO ME

NINE CHRISTMAS PUZZLES

At the North Pole we seven gnomes fight over the Christmas puzzle books to see if we can catch one another out . . . everyone except Gnigel who sleeps under the bed because he's a little potty . . . Anyway, see if you can work out the following puzzles. The answers are on page 92.

Riddles

1. What travels over water, under water but doesn't touch water?

2. How do you get down from an elephant?

3. If there are two flies in an airing cupboard, which one is in the army?

4. What is 96 years old, walks with a stick and lives at the North Pole?

5. What tool do you use to flatten a ghost?

WRITE YOUR ANSWERS HERE.

1. _____

2. _____

3. _____

4. _____

5. _____

Word-search

6. Find the word that describes Father Christmas when he can't find his thermal knickers on Christmas morning.

```
G  R  U  M  P  Y
x  N  A  S  T  Y
F  U  R  I  O  U
A  N  G  R  Y  S
F  I  E  R  C  E
S  N  A  P  P  Y
```

7.

Spot the difference 1.

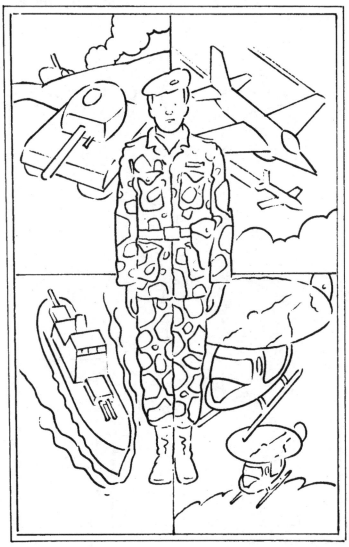

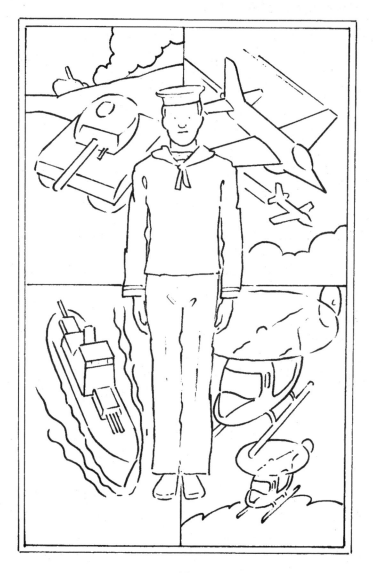

8.
Spot the difference 2.

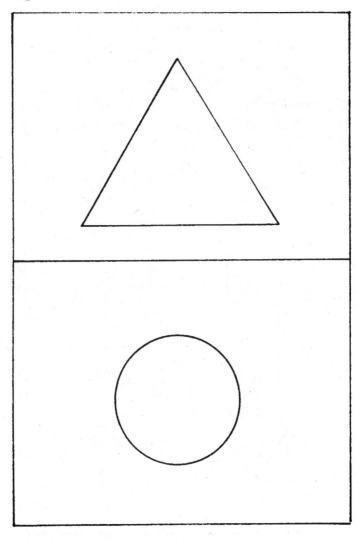

Test your knowledge

9. General Knowledge: Name three foods that begin with 't'.

10. History: Where was Ann Boleyn beheaded?

11. Biology: What is the largest mouse in the world?

12. Mathematics: If 2's company and 3's a crowd what are 4 and 5?

13. Physics: What do you call a snowman with a sun tan?

14. Geography: Where was King Solomon's temple?

15. Christmas: How many 'A' levels has Father Christmas got?

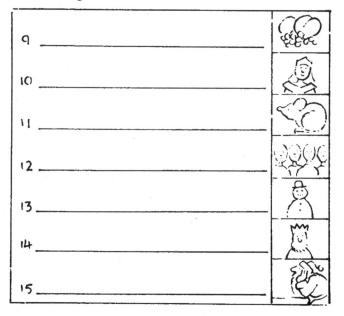

Test your brain power

16. What seven letters did Father Christmas say when he looked in Gnigel's earhole?

17. What two letters did Father Christmas say when he looked at Gnora's rotten tooth?

18. What four letters did the hungry horse say?

Master-mind bender

19. Thirty days hath September, April, June and November, all the rest have thirty-one *but* . . . how many months have twenty-eight days?

AND NOW, TURN THE PAGE TO CHECK YOUR ANSWERS . . .

Answers

Riddles:

1. A man on a bridge with a bucket of water on his head.
2. You don't get down from an elephant – you get it from a swan.
3. The one on the tank.
4. A little cold lady.
5. A spirit level.

Word-search:

6. The answer is "x" – because he's a little cross.

Spot the difference **1**:

7. The difference is that you can't dip a sailor in your soft-boiled egg.

Spot the difference **2**:

8. There is no difference; they are both pictures of Father Christmas' house in a snowstorm.

Test your knowledge:

9. Tin of plums, tin of peaches and tin of peas.
10. Just below the chin.
11. The hippo-poto-mouse.
12. Nine.
13. A puddle.
14. On his forehead.
15. None. He just has "Ho! Ho! Ho!" levels.

Test your brain-power:

16. O.I.C.U.R.M.T.

17. D.K.

18. If you said M.T.G.G. you'd be *wrong*! The answer is *nothing* – 'cos horses can't talk, stupid!

Master-mind-bender

19. They all have! Ho! Ho! Ho!

Now Check Your Score

20: Dirty rotten cheat! There were only nineteen questions.

10–19: Clever clogs.

1–9: Thicko!

0: Look out, Gnigel, someone out there's as dim as you!

ON THE TENTH DAY OF CHRISTMAS
MY TRUE LOVE SENT TO ME

TEN CHRISTMAS STORIES

When Christmas is over we gnomes like to sit around the fire and tell our favourite stories.

FATHER CHRISTMAS:	Gnigel, what's your favourite story?
GNIGEL:	Er . . . the one where the three creatures are scared of the Big Bad Wolf and they grow on trees!
FATHER CHRISTMAS:	Oh, you mean "The Three Little Figs".

FATHER CHRISTMAS:	And what's your favourite Christmas story, Gneil?
GNEIL:	Oh, the one about the ghost that steals the porridge!
FATHER CHRISTMAS:	Oh, you mean "Ghoul-di-locks"!

GNELLIE:	I like the story about the girl who steals from the rich and gives it all to Granny.
FATHER CHRISTMAS:	Ah, that's "Little Red Robin Hood"!
GNORMAN:	My favourite is the famous film about the man who casts spells in the middle of a swamp.
FATHER CHRISTMAS:	That's called "The Wizard of Ooze"!
GNOCKER:	So what's your favourite story, Father Christmas?
FATHER CHRISTMAS:	I like the story about Floella, my Christmas Fairy, and the little brown hare.
GNOCKER:	Tell us that one, Father Christmas.
FATHER CHRISTMAS:	Are you sitting comfortably? Then I'll begin –

Once upon a time, in the Christmas Tree Forest there lived the Christmas fairies. They spent most of their time practising sitting on top of Christmas trees. There was just one rule they had to stick to . . . it was strictly forbidden for a fairy to kiss anyone!

The trouble was that Floella was a wicked little fairy.

One day Harry the Hare was hopping through the forest when he saw Floella sitting on top of a toadstool, combing her hair. Floella said, "Hello, handsome, give us a kiss!"

Harry the Hare was shocked. "Father Christmas doesn't allow it!" he gasped. "Anyone caught kissing a fairy will be turned straight away into a Goon!"

But Floella tickled his ears – just the way hares love – and whispered, "Don't worry, we won't be caught!"

Harry the Hare trembled with fear and excitement. He looked carefully over his furry brown shoulder, saw that no one was looking . . . and *kissed* Floella the fairy!

Suddenly there was a FLASH, a C*R*A*S*H and a mighty WHOOSH!!! of wind. Through the magic of the Christmas Tree Forest Harry the Hare found himself in the court of Father Christmas!

And Father Christmas was furious! "Harry the Hare! You have been found guilty of kissing a forest fairy! Have you anything to say?"

"I never meant to!" Harry the Hare snivelled. "If you let me off I promise I'll never do it again . . . just please, please!! PLEASE!!! don't turn me into a Goon!"

Father Christmas took pity on the pathetic creature and said, "I'll give you one more chance . . . just one more!"

Suddenly there was a FLASH, a C*R*A*S*H and a mighty WHOOSH!!! of wind. Harry the

Hare found himself back in the forest. And there, combing her hair on a toadstool was Floella the Fairy.

"Hiya, handsome," she whispered. "Give us a kiss!"

Harry the Hare was horrified! "Certainly not!" he cried. But when she tickled his ears his legs turned to jelly and he started to tremble. "Oooh! No! I'll be turned into a Goon!"

"For one little kiss from me it's worth it!" Floella murmured.

And Harry the Hare gave in. He kissed the fairy.

Suddenly there was a FLASH, a C*R*A*S*H and a mighty WHOOSH!!! of wind. Once again Harry the Hare found himself in front of the furious Father Christmas!

"You foolish hare!" Father Christmas roared. "You have had your chance! Guards! Take him away – turn him into a Goon tomorrow!"

Harry the Hare hung his head and let himself be led away. As he reached the door of the court he turned to all the gnomes and forest creatures and said tearfully . . .

"Ah, well, that's life! Hare today . . . and Goon tomorrow!"

Now Gnigel's favourite story was about Gneil . . .

One day Gnigel went for a walk to the North Pole to feed the penguins. Who should he meet there but Gneil! And Gneil had a sack of green and purple sand and he was scattering it all over the snow.

"Gneil! What on earth are you doing?" Gnigel asked.

"I'm scattering this magic green and purple sand," Gneil told him.

"But *why* are you scattering green and purple sand?" Gnigel demanded.

"To keep the crocodiles away, of course!" Gneil told him.

Gnigel gasped. "But there *aren't* any crocodiles at the North Pole!"

Gneil grinned happily. "I know. Great stuff isn't it?"

Gnora loved to hear a ghost story at Christmas. She particularly loved the one about the ghostly dog . . .

There was once a dog who died and came back to haunt the street he lived in.

He loved scaring cats. One Christmas Eve, just about midnight, he'd scared a fat black moggy and sent it howling home. The ghost dog was so happy he wagged his ghost-tail and wagged his ghost-tail . . . until it dropped off!

The tail lay sadly on the ground. The dog picked it up in his mouth but couldn't reach behind to stick it back on. Midnight was striking and people were flocking to the pub that was open late. The dog wandered into the pub and jumped on to the bar.

"Excuse me," the dog said politely. "But do you think you could stick my tail back on?"

The landlord turned and looked at the clock on the wall behind the bar. "Oh, sorry mate," he sighed. "But, you see, I'm not permitted to re-tail spirits after midnight!"

Gnorman liked ghost stories too. But his favourite was about the Christmas wrapping string . . .

One Christmas Eve, when all the presents had been wrapped, there were just three pieces of string left.

"You know, we'll probably just be thrown on the fire," String No. 1 said.

"Or in the bin!" String No.2 moaned.

"We can't have that!" String No. 3 cried.

"So what can we do?" the other two pieces asked.

"Let's go out for a meal!" String No. 3 suggested.

And off they went down to the "Greasy Penguin Cafe". It was packed with Christmas revellers. String No. 1 said, "Right, lads, what'll we eat?"

"I'd like some tomato soup," said String No.2.

"And how about stuffed turkey to follow ... and we could have Christmas pudding for afters," said String No. 3.

String No. 1 went to the counter and said, "Three tomato soups, three stuffed turkeys and three Christmas puddings, my good man!"

The waiter took one look at him and said, "Push off, shorty. I don't serve pieces of string ... and you're just a piece of string!"

String No. 1 went back to the others. "He refused to serve me!"

String No. 2 asked, "Did you say 'please'?"

"No," admitted String No. 1.

"Then let me try!"

String No.2 went to the bar and said, "Three tomato soups, three stuffed turkeys and three Christmas puddings, *please*."

But the waiter replied, "Push off, shorty. I don't serve pieces of string ... and you're just a piece of string!"

String No.2 went back to the others to report

his failure. "Here, lads, let me try," String No.3 offered. But, before he went to the bar he tied a knot in the top of his head and fluffed the end out till he looked like a piece of punk string.

He went up to the bar. "Three tomato soups, three stuffed turkeys and three Christmas puddings, please!"

The waiter looked at him and sighed, "Push off, shorty. I don't serve pieces of string . . . and you're just a piece of string!"

And String No.3 replied, "No. I'm a frayed knot!"

But Gnellie has my favourite Christmas story of all . . .

Once upon a time there was a little girl who wanted a kitten for Christmas. Now, her mother couldn't buy a kitten and parcel it up for Christmas Day, so she bought it a week before Christmas and gave it to the little girl. "You're getting your Christmas present a week early this year," her mother explained and handed over the fluffy little tabby kitten. "Is that what you want?"

The little girl, whose name was Kitty, said, "It's wonderful, mother . . . just what I wanted. There's just one thing wrong!"

"What's that?" her mother asked.

"Well, it has a cute little claw on the outside of every paw and a cute little claw on the inside of every paw – but the poor little thing has no claws at all in the middle of its paws!"

Her mother smiled. "Don't worry, Kitty . . . when you wake up on Christmas morning you'll find the claws are there."

Now Kitty loved her kitten dearly, but she worried about those claws in the middle of its paws. The days passed and there wasn't even a hint, a clue or an inkling of claws in the middle of its paws!

When Christmas Eve arrived and there was still no sign, Kitty went to her mother and asked again, "Are you absolutely *sure* that the kitten will have its middle claws tomorrow? There's only a few hours to go and there's not a hint or a clue or an inkling as to claws as far as I can see!"

"Wait till you wake up on Christmas morning," her mother smiled and went on stuffing the turkey.

So Kitty went to sleep a worried girl. And when she woke up on Christmas morning she ignored the presents in her stocking and rushed downstairs to look at her little kitten.

She was astounded, amazed and just a little surprised to see that her kitten had four claws on every paw! The middle ones had appeared as if by magic.

Kitty rushed to her parent's bedroom. "Mummy, Mummy! The kitten has grown its middle claws!"

"Of course it has," her mother grinned.

"But how did you *know*?" Kitty demanded.

Her father rolled over sleepily and sighed, "Oh, Kitty, everybody knows . . . that Centre-claws always comes at Christmas!"

ON THE ELEVENTH DAY OF CHRISTMAS
MY TRUE LOVE SENT TO ME

ELEVEN CHRISTMAS JOKES

As I told you, Gnellie is a gnome who's always feeling poorly . . .

GNELLIE: Doctor, doctor, I keep thinking
I'm a Christmas bell!

DOCTOR: Just take these pills – and, if they
don't work, give me a ring!

GNELLIE:	Doctor, doctor, with all the excitement of Christmas I can't sleep.
DOCTOR:	Try lying on the edge of your bed . . . you'll soon drop off!
GNELLIE:	Doctor, doctor, Father Christmas gives us oranges every Christmas. Now I think I'm turning into an orange!
DOCTOR:	Have you tried playing squash?
GNELLIE:	Will that make me fit?
DOCTOR:	No. To get a gnome fit you'll have to go to an elf farm.
GNELLIE:	What else should I do?
DOCTOR:	You have to eat your greens – put a bit of colour in your cheeks!
GNELLIE:	Who wants green cheeks!
DOCTOR:	Don't worry. You'll live to be a hundred!
GNELLIE:	I was a hundred last Christmas.
DOCTOR:	There you are! What did I tell you! Now just breathe out four times.
GNELLIE:	You want to check my lungs?
DOCTOR:	No. I want to clean my glasses.
GNELLIE:	Doctor, doctor, I feel as tense as an elastic band.

DOCTOR:	Snap out of it.
GNELLIE:	It's fear of going into that little dark toy cupboard of Father Christmas'.
DOCTOR:	You're suffering from Claustrophobia.
GNELLIE:	And I keep imagining I'm a snow-covered field!
DOCTOR:	What *has* come over you?
GNELLIE:	Two sleighs, three polar bears and a flock of penguins!

GNELLIE: Doctor, doctor, I've got a bad stomach.

DOCTOR: Keep your coat buttoned up and no one will notice.

GNELLIE: But doctor, I think I need glasses!

DOCTOR: You certainly do. I'm the baker!

GNELLIE: Doctor, what do you give someone who feels sick?

DOCTOR: Plenty of room.

GNELLIE: Doctor, doctor, will this ointment cure my spots?

DOCTOR: I'm not making any rash promises.

| GNELLIE: | My problem is that I keep stealing things when I go Christmas shopping. Can you give me something for it! |
| DOCTOR: | Try this medicine . . . and if it doesn't work come back and bring me a new video camera. |

| DOCTOR: | Nurse! I want to operate. Take this patient to the theatre. |
| GNELLIE: | Ooh! Good! I love a nice pantomime at Christmas! |

Gnellie went to the doctor with a reindeer on her head.

"Gosh!" the doctor exclaimed. "You have a real problem there!"

"I certainly have!" the reindeer moaned. "Get this rotten gnome from under my feet!"

And talking about Father Christmas' reindeer you really should know their names.

| GNIGEL: | What does Father Christmas call that three-legged reindeer? |
| GNORA: | Eileen. |

| GNORMAN: | And what does he call that reindeer with no eyes? |
| GNELLIE: | No-eyed-deer! |

113

GNEIL:	And what do you call the reindeer with cotton wool in his ears?
GNOCKER:	Call him anything you like – he won't hear you!
GNEIL:	What do you call the reindeer with one eye higher than the other?
GNOCKER:	Isaiah!
GNORMAN:	What about the reindeer with only one eye that's got no legs?
GNELLIE:	Still no-eye-deer.
GNANCY:	What's the name of the reindeer with three humps on its back?
GNIGEL:	Humphrey, of course.
GNANCY:	And that black and blue reindeer?
GNIGEL:	Bruce.

114

GNORA: Tell me, Father Christmas, how did Rudolph get that song written about him?

FATHER CHRISTMAS: Well, it's a long story . . . Once upon a time there was a king in Lapland called Rudolph. He had bright ginger hair so his people called him Rudolph the Red.

Now Rudolph the Red was bad-tempered and argued a lot. He gave his poor wife, Gertrude the Green, a terrible time. No matter what she said he had to argue.

One winter's day Gertrude the Green looked out of the palace window and said, "Oh, dear, it's snowing again. You'll have to clear the footpath before mother comes to tea."

"Humph!" Rudolph the Red grunted. He didn't fancy shifting snow and he didn't want

Gertrude the Green's mother coming to tea. "That's not snow. It's rain!" he argued.

"But it's white and fluffy and drifting," Gertrude the Green tried to tell him.

Rudolph the Red hid behind his newspaper and snapped, "It's rain!"

Gertrude the Green became quite angry. "Gertrude the Green knows snow, darling!"

"Yes," retorted her husband. "And Rudolph the Red knows rain, dear!"

"What a great title for a song!" Gertrude the Green exclaimed.

Of course Rudolph is the most famous of Father Christmas' reindeer. Not many people know that he's always getting lost. In fact, he was lost when Gnorman the Gnome first came across him . . .

Gnorman the Gnome went to Father Christmas and said, "Father Christmas! I've just found this red-nosed reindeer wandering around outside."

"Ah!" Father Christmas exclaimed. "Take him down to the Greenland zoo, eh Gnorman?"

And off went Gnorman.

But the next day Father Christmas saw Gnorman with the red-nosed reindeer trotting behind. "I thought I told you to take that reindeer to the zoo, Gnorman!"

"Yes, I took him yesterday," Gnorman answered. "And he liked it so much that I'm taking him to the circus today and the cinema tomorrow!"

GNELLIE:	You don't see many reindeer in zoos, do you?
GNANCY:	No. They can't afford the admission.
FATHER CHRISTMAS:	Rudolph the red-nosed reindeer's gone missing again, Gnocker. Put a "Missing" advert in the local paper!
GNOCKER:	Don't be daft. Reindeer can't read!
GNANCY:	Tell me, Gnigel, how would you get four reindeer in a car?
GNIGEL:	I don't know, Gnancy, how *would* you get four reindeer in a car?
GNANCY:	Two in the front and two in the back!
GNIGEL:	And how do you get four polar bears in a car?
GNANCY:	Take the reindeer out first.

Most people imagine that it's easy flying through the air with Father Christmas to deliver all those presents. But, if truth were told, Father Christmas is not too good a driver and we have some pretty scary times, I can tell you . . .

I remember when Father Christmas first passed his sleigh-driving test. He came skidding down in front of the toy factory.

"Have you passed?" Gneil asked.

Father Christmas pointed proudly to the front of the sleigh. "See for yourself!" he called proudly. "No-el plates!"

He was a terrible driver at first. We had a reindeer who always crashed . . . so we called him "Rex".

One snowy night Father Christmas checked the sledge. "Are my indicators working, Gnora?" he asked, flicking the switch.

"Yes – no – yes – no – yes – no – yes – no!" Gnora replied.

"I think I'll have to take this sledge for a service," Father Christmas sighed.

"You'd never get it up the church steps," Gnellie told him.

He'd gone no further than Greenland motorway when he broke down. He flagged down a passing motorist and asked, "Can you help me fix my sledge?"

"Sorry," the motorist replied. "I'm not a mechanic – I'm a chiropodist."

"Well, can you give me a toe?"

Now Father Christmas was late. He managed to fix his sleigh, and raced across the sky till he was stopped by a policeman in a helicopter – from the Flying Squad! "I have reason to believe you were exceeding the speed limit,"

the policeman said.

"*I* wasn't!" Father Christmas lied. "But I passed two fellers who were!"

"I'm sorry, sir," the policeman went on. "I'll have to ask you to accompany me!"

Father Christmas took a guitar from a sack and said, "Certainly, officer, what would you like to sing?"

"I'd like you to accompany me to the station," the policeman said.

"Why? Are you catching a train?"

"I mean the police station," the policeman said.

"Where's that?" Father Christmas asked.

"In the Avenue."

"Which avenue?"

"'Ello, 'ello, 'ello, let's-be avenue!"

At the police station Father Christmas was asked if he knew he was going up a one-way street.

"But I was only going one way!" he argued.

"Didn't you see the arrows?"

"Arrows! I didn't even see the Indians!"

"And what gear were you in when you hit those penguins?"

"Oh," Father Christmas told him. "The usual gear. Red suit, trimmed with white fur, and black boots!"

"I'll have to lock you up for the night, Father Christmas," the policeman said.

"What's the charge?"

"Oh, there's no charge. It's all part of the service!"

Father Christmas was so late delivering presents that he ran out of reindeer juice and started to crash-land.

"May-day! May-day!" Father Christmas cried into his radio. "Come in, control! I am crashing! I repeat, I am crashing!"

"Control here, control here!" came the reply. "Father Christmas, please state your height and position!"

"Er, five foot eight and about six foot behind Rudolph's bum!"

Father Christmas was late home that year. He let the reindeer back into their stalls to play . . .

| GNOCKER: | What game do reindeer play in their stalls? |
| GNEIL: | Stable-tennis, of course! |

Gnora wanted to let Rudolph into the house . . .

| GNELLIE: | Keep that reindeer out of the house! It's full of fleas! |
| GNORA: | You'd better stay out of the house, Rudolph – it's full of fleas. |

So Gnora took Rudolph back to the stalls and they pulled Christmas crackers with the world's worst jokes . . .

GNORA: What reindeer can jump higher than a house?

RUDOLPH: They all can! Houses can't jump!

GNORA: Why are Father Christmas' reindeer like a cricket match?

RUDOLPH: Because they're both stopped by the rein.

GNORA: What has antlers, pulls Father Christmas' sleigh and is made of cement?

RUDOLPH: I don't know.

GNORA: A reindeer!

RUDOLPH: What about the cement?

GNORA: I just threw that in to make it hard.

GNORA:	What's the difference between a reindeer and a snowball?
RUDOLPH:	They're both brown, except the snowball.
GNORA:	Why don't Prancer and Dancer and the other reindeer overtake you, Rudolph?
RUDOLPH:	Because they don't believe in passing the buck!
GNORA:	What bird can write under the Arctic Ocean?
RUDOLPH:	A ball-point pen-guin.

GNORA: Why don't the polar bears eat the penguins?

RUDOLPH: Because they can't get the silver paper off!

GNORA: One last reindeer joke, then it's your turn, Rudolph. What has antlers and loves cheese?

RUDOLPH: Mickey Moose!

RUDOLPH: What did the beaver say to the Christmas tree?

GNORA: It's been nice gnawing you!

RUDOLPH: What bird gasps and pants at the North Pole?

GNORA: A puffin.

RUDOLPH: How do you get milk from a polar bear?

GNORA: Rob its fridge and run like mad.

RUDOLPH: What do you call Christmas ducks?

GNORA: Christmas quackers.

RUDOLPH: And what happens when they fly upside down?

GNORA: They quack up!

RUDOLPH: What do you call a cow at the North Pole?

GNORA: An eski-moo!

RUDOLPH: I'll bet you can't tell me where my mother comes from!

GNORA: Alaska!

RUDOLPH: That's cheating!

IGMOO

ON THE TWELFTH DAY OF CHRISTMAS
MY TRUE LOVE SENT TO ME

TWELVE FATHER CHRISTMASES

When all the presents are delivered, Father Christmas likes to relax. In fact he goes to bed after Christmas and sets the alarm for Easter. And he doesn't like to be disturbed . . .

GNIGEL: Father Christmas, there's a bird at the door with a yellow bill.

FATHER CHRISTMAS: I don't care what colour its bill is, I'm not paying it!

GNORA: Father Christmas, there's a man at the door with a wooden leg!

FATHER CHRISTMAS: Tell him to hop it!

So, you see, Father Christmas is far from perfect . . .

GNORMAN: What rides a sleigh, gives lots of presents and has plenty of faults?

GNELLIE: Santa Flaws.

GNEIL: I remember when a lady wanted a new nightie for Christmas and asked Father Christmas for something cool and white.

GNOCKER: So he gave her a fridge!

GNEIL: And the time Father Christmas buried some potatoes two metres under the North Pole with a packet of razor blades.

GNOCKER: Said he was trying to grow frozen chips.

GNORMAN: What about the time when Father Christmas ran over that lady's cat? He went to her door to apologize and said, "Do you think I could replace it?"

"I don't know," the woman sniffed. "How good are you at catching mice?"

GNOCKER: Father Christmas once came down in the South Seas and had to deliver presents on the back of a huge fish.

GNEIL: An accident?

GNOCKER: No. He did it on porpoise.

GNIGEL: Then there was the time Father Christmas lost his underpants.

GNORA: That's how he got the name Saint Knickerless!

GNELLIE: Is it true that Father Christmas fought for Drake against the Spanish Armada?

GNEIL: He was certainly at Plymouth Ho-ho-ho!

GNANCY: That reminds me. What goes Ho-squelch, Ho-squelch, Ho-squelch?

GNOCKER: Father Christmas with snow in his wellies.

GNANCY: And what goes Ho-squelch, Ho-squelch, Ho-squelch, BANG?

GNOCKER: Father Christmas with snow in his wellies in a minefield!

GNANCY: And what goes Oh! Oh! Oh?

GNOCKER: Father Christmas walking backwards.

Father Christmas is very easy to spot . . . fat, with snowy hair and a red suit, flying round the sky on a sleigh. But surprisingly few people see him.

GNIGEL: A group of mountain climbers once heard Father Christmas go past.

GNORMAN: They must have had sharp ears!

GNIGEL: Of course. They were mountain-ears!

GNORA: Mind you, Father Christmas has tried to do something about his bald patch. He went to Doctor Weirdly to get a hair restorer. The doctor said, "I have some good news and some bad news! The bad news is that I can't make hair grow on your head . . . but the good news is that I can shrink your head so the little bit you have got fits!"

GNELLIE:	And of course he gets his clothes cheap.
GNEIL:	He certainly gets them for a ridiculous figure.
GNELLIE:	Did you know that Father Christmas once climbed on a "Speak-your-weight" machine?
GNEIL:	And the machine said "One at a time please!"

We gnomes can be very cruel about Father Christmas at times. Last Christmas he was asked to do a lot of television adverts. When he got back to the North Pole he asked us:

"Did you see me?"
"On and off," we said.
"And how did you like me?"
"Off!" we told him.

But Father Christmas' worst gnome is Gnigel . . .
because Gnigel is so stupid. He always has been.

GNORMAN: He thought "Illegal" was a sick bird.

GNELLIE: He thought "Backgammon" was a pig's behind.

GNEIL: He had a zebra and he called it "Spot".

GNOCKER: When he was asked to do a bird impression he ate a plate full of worms!

GNANCY: And when a cake recipe said "Separate two eggs" he put one in the kitchen and one in the bedroom.

Gnigel was trouble at school . . .

TEACHER: Gnellie, what is a comet?

GNELLIE: A star with a tail, sir.

TEACHER: Gnigel, name a comet.

GNIGEL: Er . . . Lassie, sir!

TEACHER: Unlock the piano lid, Gnigel.

GNIGEL: I can't, sir. All the keys are inside!

TEACHER: Gnigel, use the word "Gladiator" in a sentence.

GNIGEL: My chicken stopped laying eggs so I'm glad-i-ator!

TEACHER:	Gnigel. You have your wellies on the wrong feet!
GNIGEL:	They're the only feet I've got, sir!
TEACHER:	Show our guest the door, Gnigel.
GNIGEL:	It's that wooden thing over there, missus!

And Gnigel was trouble when he left school . . .

He went to work for the North Pole weather service. His first caller said, "What's the chance of a shower?"

Gnigel replied, "Fine if you have enough hot water!"

So he went to work for a glazier. The trouble was he couldn't tell putty from toothpaste. Not only did his teeth stick together but all the windows he fitted fell out!

Gnigel went to work for a forester. "What's the outside of a Christmas tree called?" the forester asked.

"Dunno," Gnigel replied.

"Bark," the forester said.

"O.K. Woof! Woof!" Gnigel went.

He tried to become a long distance swimmer. But he got halfway across the English Channel, decided he couldn't make it and swam back.

Even when he had good luck he was too daft to make the most of it . . .

One day Gnigel met a Christmas fairy in the forest. The fairy liked the look of Gnigel so she said, "Little Gnome, I grant you three wishes!"

"Ooh! I'd like a can of Coke!" Gnigel gasped.

"Your wish is my command!" the fairy said and a large can of Coke appeared in front of Gnigel. It was delicious. "What is more," the fairy said. "It is magic. Every time it empties, it fills itself up again! Now what are your next two wishes?"

"That can's brill!" Gnigel cried. "I'll have another two of those!"

He once went to the doctor. "I've got a splitting headache," he complained . . . so the doctor gave him a tube of glue.

"How long can a gnome live without a brain?" Gnigel asked.

"I don't know. How old are you?"

"I keep thinking I'm a chicken," Gnigel complained.

"I can cure that," the doctor offered.

"Oh no!" Gnigel cried. "My mother needs the eggs!"

"My mother says she has an IQ of 100," Gnigel claimed. "What's an IQ of 100?"

"A hundred gnomes like you," the doctor explained.

Gnigel took his comb to the dentist because its teeth were falling out!

Gnigel went to a mind-reader – she charged him half-price.

Then Gnigel came to work for Father Christmas . . .
The other gnomes made fun of him at first . . .

GNORMAN: I say, I say, I say. What's stupid and sees just as well from either end?

GNEIL: Gnigel in a blindfold!

GNIGEL: Here. What's the idea of telling everyone I'm an idiot?

GNORMAN: Sorry. I didn't know it was a secret.

GNIGEL: You must think I'm a perfect fool!

GNORMAN: Nobody's perfect . . . but you come pretty close!

Mind you, Gneil was nearly as bad . . .

One day Gnigel had the job of making toy boxes. He was hammering nails into the sides of the box . . . but Gneil noticed he was throwing half the nails away.

"Here, Gnigel, why are you throwing those nails away?"

"The heads are on the wrong end," Gnigel explained.

"Don't be stupid!" Gneil cried. "Those are for the other side!"

So Gnigel gave Father Christmas a big problem when he came to work . . .

One day Gnigel phoned Father Christmas to say he couldn't come in to work because he'd lost his voice!

One day Gnigel was very late for work. He'd
been crossing a cow-meadow when his beret
had blown off. He'd tried twenty on his head
before he found the right one.

FATHER CHRISTMAS:	Gnigel! Call me a taxi!
GNIGEL:	You're a taxi, Father Christmas!
GNIGEL:	I've had a slight accident with your sleigh, Father Christmas!
FATHER CHRISTMAS:	Oh no! That sleigh was in mint condition!
GNIGEL:	That's all right . . . now it's a mint with a hole!
FATHER CHRISTMAS:	Gnigel, I thought I asked you to go out there and clear the snow!
GNIGEL:	I'm on my way, Father Christmas.
FATHER CHRISTMAS:	But you only have one welly on!
GNIGEL:	That's all right! There's only one foot of snow!

*But generally Father Christmas and the gnomes
have a merry Christmas at the North Pole . . .*

Last year we all bought him a special present –
guess what?

What's fat and jolly and runs on eight
wheels?

Father Christmas on roller skates!

139

And why does Father Christmas go down chimneys?

Because they soot him.

And before you know it we are having a very happy new year . . .

Gnock! Gnock!
Who's there?
Father.
Father who?
Fa-ther sake of auld lang syne!

Then Father Christmas can sleep the rest of winter and come out in spring to tend his garden . . .

What does Father Christmas do in the summer?
Hoe, hoe, hoe!

THE GREAT
FATHER
CHRISTMAS
ROBBERY

When you're ripping open presents at the break
of Christmas Day,
Don't forget the kind old man in red and white.
Don't forget the man who brought you all that joy
and happiness.
While you slept he worked so hard all through the
night.

You may think he has an easy life just dropping
off your toys,
You may think he has to work just once a year.
But old Santa has had problems of the sort you'd
never guess,
Open up this book and read of them in here . . .

'Twas the night before Christmas Eve, and all through the house, something was stirring . . . and it wasn't a mouse!

Or even a moose!

More like a reindeer.

I stuck my head out of my bedroom window and looked up. There, on my roof, was a reindeer, chewing my television aerial. And behind the reindeer a sleigh loaded with presents. It was just like a visit from Father Christmas . . . but why was he a day too early?

I crept downstairs and peered around the living room door. There he was! A fat little feller with a bushy white beard, a poppy-red suit and dark glasses. He was filling his sack with some of the presents that lay under the Christmas tree. I know I should have gone back to bed, but I was so thrilled at seeing Father Christmas that I hid and watched.

The little man felt each parcel carefully. "Aha!" he chuckled. "A doll!" and popped it in his sack. I thought he might laugh "Ho! Ho! Ho!" as he headed for the chimney. Instead he giggled "Hee! Hee! Hee!"

I tiptoed back to my bed. I lay down. I jumped up. Hey! That fat little man was *filling* his sack. He wasn't *leaving* presents . . . he was *stealing* them. I looked out of my window just in time to see the thieving Father Christmas and his thieving reindeer fly off into the night with a "Hee! Hee! Hee!"

"Help!" I cried. "There's a pair of nickers on my roof!"

I knew the police could never catch them – not unless I called the flying squad.

Someone who looked like Father Christmas was out to ruin the day for all the children. Someone had to stop him . . . someone like me! But where did I start? Where would I get help? Where were my clean socks?

This was a case for that great detective . . . Sherlock Gnomes!

I looked up his number in Yellow Pages . . .

GNOME & AWAY
Soap Manufacturers   Australia 321

GNOME & DRY
Towel Manufacturers   Bath 123

GNOME MOST THINGS
School   Eton 213

GNOME SICK
Hospital for little people Illverness 231

GNOME WORK
Builders for gnomeless people Brixton 312

GNOMING PIGEONS
Messenger Service   Nestminster 321

GNOMES SHERLOCK
Greatest living detective   Clueless 123

HOLMES SHERLOCK
Greatest dead detective   Baker St 21b.

I called the great man at once . . .

I waited five hours! Suddenly there was a tap on the door.

I peered through the window and saw a funny looking little feller . . . deerstalker hat, hooked pipe under his chin and a violin smouldering in his mouth.

I opened the door and there stood the famous Sherlock Gnomes. The great man himself . . . just like in the pictures . . . but smaller.

I quickly told him my story . . .

So we set off on the trail of Father Christmas. Snow drifted up to Sherlock's chin – it wasn't very deep. We didn't have snow shoes but we strapped a couple of tennis racquets onto our feet.

"Sorry I don't have the real snow shoes," I told him.

"Never mind," the great man sighed, "these racquets will have to serve."

I wouldn't have known where to start searching for a burglar but Sherlock insisted on following tracks along the road. . . .

The great detective was right, of course. What else could leave deep straight tracks in the snow and jingle along like that?

Well, a tram for one thing! But a man like Sherlock Gnomes isn't the sort to be put off by a battered nose and a broken violin.

We limped after the tram and caught it as it stopped for a zebra crossing. Luckily for us the zebra took its time. I bought two tickets for the North Pole and sat down for the long cold journey.

As we rattled along Sherlock told me his cunning plan. He decided that we needed to know more about this Father Christmas character. Where did he come from? How did he get the job? And what made him turn crooked? But, for Sherlock the most burning question of all was . . .

Luckily we found a snack-bar that was open . . .

SAM 'n' ELLA'S SNACK-BAR

Bacon & Penguin Eggs — 1.00 (clean plate 20 extra)

Deep-Fried Igloo — 1.00 (per bottle)

Reindeer-food — 10.00 (per bag - vely deer indeed).

Frozen chips — 1.00 (home-grown mashed potato)

M°Whale Burgers (in whale fat) — 1.00 (for cry babies - eat them + blubber)

Ice burgers — 1.00 (A Titanic snack)

Turkey Soup — 1.00 (for gobblers)

Eskimo Milk — 1.00 (from eskimoos)

Ice Cream Surprise — 1.00

TRY ELLA'S SPECIAL POTATOES! SHE CROSSED A POTATO WITH A SPONGE - THE POTATO TASTES AWFUL. BUT IT'S GREAT WHEN YOU MOP UP YOUR GRAVY!

So we knocked on Ella's door . . .

I wouldn't say Ella's snack-bar was scruffy but I'll swear I saw a skunk with a clothes-peg on its nose. There was a lot of food on the menu . . . and even more on the tables and the floor!

"That soup looks like dishwater!" I complained.

Ella gave a sickly grin. "Oh, dear!" she cried.

"I think I've just washed the cups in chicken noodle soup!"

We sat at a table with a spotted cloth – spots of stale food mostly – and ordered.

SHERLOCK: Ella! Ella! This egg's bad!

ELLA: Don't blame me! I only laid the table.

SHERLOCK: Then give me two Ice Cream Surprises!

ELLA: Surprise! Surprise!

Sherlock Gnomes wasted no time in questioning the woman . . .

So we left the snack-bar and set off on the search for the real Father Christmas and to solve the mystery of the missing dolls. We had just twelve hours to find a thief and return the loot. Twelve hours to save Christmas for all the children in the world!

The North Pole houses were more cheerful than Ella's cafe. Brightly painted wooden cottages with carved shutters keeping out the cold wind. We found Grandfather Claus's house thanks to Sherlock's amazing powers of deduction again. (His name was printed inside the wellies that

stood on the doorstep!) It looked lovely and warm in that cottage.

Grandfather Claus was a jolly old man. So old that even his wrinkles had wrinkles. He was fat, but not so fat as an elephant, and his nose was red – but not so red as an elephant either. As we went in a cat jumped down from his lap. He asked us to put the cat out – I hadn't even noticed it was on fire!

163

"What brings you to the North Pole?" he asked.

"A tram!" Sherlock said quickly.

SHERLOCK: We've come to ask you about your son.

GRANDFATHER: Me *Sun*? I never read it! I only read the *North Pole Times*.

WATSON: No! Your s-o-n. Son!

GRANDFATHER: Ah! You mean our Santa Claus!

SHERLOCK: Is that what you call him? How did he come to get a name like that?

GRANDFATHER: I'm glad you asked me that. It's a funny story . . .

So he told us . . .

"Not a lot of people know this, but Santa Claus was born at a very early age. In fact he was born a full twelve months before his first birthday. An unusual baby, though. It was the white beard and whiskers that did it . . ."

"We were so proud!" Grandfather Claus told us. "And Santa was a wonderful baby! Everybody loved him. We entered him for the 'North Pole Beautiful Baby Competition' and, would you believe it, he won!"

But we still wanted to know how he got the name Santa Claus . . .

Grandfather Claus told us it was all due to a mistake at the christening. It seems the vicar was deaf as an on-duty traffic warden. At the same time Grandmother Claus was worrying about what to send her Auntie Gladys for Christmas.

VICAR:	I name this child . . . er . . . .
GRANDMOTHER:	What shall we send Aunt Gladys?
VICAR:	I name this child . . .
GRANDFATHER:	Send her clothes!

And that was how Father Christmas got his name! Of course Grandfather Claus wasn't too happy about it, but it was too late to change it. Santa was stuck with the name.

He smiled as he remembered, "Still, it could have been worse."

"How?" Sherlock asked.

"You should have seen what happened to the next kid they gave him for christening!" the old man chuckled.

"What happened?" I asked.

"Well, his mam had drunk a bottle of pop before she went to the church . . ." Grandfather Claus explained.

Grandfather Claus told us that Santa Claus was the most popular boy in the school. . . .

Well, it isn't every day you share a desk with a white-bearded friend, is it? Of course !Burp! Pardon was white-bearded too – but !Burp! was the nastiest, meanest white-bearded boy you'd ever wish to meet. He could look after himself. The other kids were scared of !Burp!. While they were playing harmless games like pulling the legs off snails !Burp! was doing much nastier things – like pulling the legs off dolls!

Grandfather Claus went on, "Then one day the school caught fire. The kids escaped by climbing down Santa Claus's beard to safety. After that he was a hero in the school. Everybody loved him. Everybody except one . . . !Burp! Pardon was jealous!"

WATSON: Did this all happen in his junior school?

SHERLOCK: They didn't have junior schools in the old days, Watson.

WATSON: So what sort of school did he go to?

ELEMENTARY MY DEAR WATSON.

YEAH... BUT WHAT SORT OF SCHOOL DID HE GO TO?

NYAAAH!

I ONLY ASKED.

"I think we need to see Santa's teacher," Sherlock murmured.

"She's called Miss Taycon ... and she lives just across the street," the old man told us. "But be careful!" he warned. "She can be a bit touchy ... and when she starts swinging her stick you have to duck pretty sharp!"

"Sherlock Gnomes is afraid of no one!" the detective said dramatically. "He boldly goes where no bold man has boldly gone before ... boldly!"

The trouble was there were several houses across the street. And they didn't have numbers ... just pictures of fruits! An orange, an apple, a cherry, a melon and a peach. This was clearly a case for the great detective's great detecting powers.

"Which one, Sherlock?" I asked.

"The one with the melon, Watson," he answered.

"Amazing, Sherlock. How could you possibly know?" I gasped.

"Melon-entry, my dear Watson," he smirked.

And, of course, he was right! When I knocked on the door an old lady answered. She was wearing a mortar board and gown and carried a cane.

I was terrified. I felt ashamed, but I had to admit it.

"I'm terrified, Sherlock!" I whispered.

"I'm not!" the bold detective said ... boldly.

"How can you stand there so calm and unafraid?" I gasped.

"Easy," he replied. "I'll just stand behind you! If she's going to hit someone then it's more likely to be you!"

"Thanks," I muttered and turned towards the towering teacher.

Eventually she let us in. We sat by her roaring fire and listened as the old lady remembered her days at North Pole Elementary School.

"Now, Phil McCavity became a famous dentist," she boasted.

"How famous?" Sherlock dared to ask.

"The best in the world. That's why they call him 'Leader of the Plaque'," she told us. "Then there was the brilliant inventor – Noah Lott," she went on, "he crossed a bed with a microwave oven. Now he can get eight hours' sleep in ten minutes."

I made the mistake of trying to interrupt her. "Miss Taycon . . ."

"How dare you!" she roared and drilled a hole in my chest with that stick of hers. "Noah was never mistaken." And the old teacher went on to tell us about the great inventor. "He invented an upside-down lighthouse."

171

Sherlock asked who would want an upside-down lighthouse!

"Someone in a submarine!" the teacher told him.

This was all very interesting, but we had just eleven hours left to save Christmas! We had to find out more about the man we'd come to find.

SHERLOCK: Er . . . madam . . . could you tell us about Santa Claus?

TEACHER: Became a chimney sweep or something, didn't he?

SHERLOCK: I think you're mistaken.

TEACHER: Of course I'm Miss Taycon – always have been!

But at last she remembered the boy with the white beard. The trouble was she didn't think much of his school work.

"Brains of a brick," she said. "Didn't he pull the legs off dolls?"

"No," I told her.

Then she went to an old cupboard and found a pile of school reports.

"Here we are!" she cried. "Claus, Santa!" and pushed the report across to Sherlock Gnomes. The great detective peered at it through his magnifying glass . . .

NORTH POLE ELEMENTARY
End of Term Report

PUPIL : CLAUS, SANTA
FORM : 1T
NO. OF PUPILS IN CLASS: 47

ENGLISH	: Rites good poems but carnt spell.	21/100
HISTORY	: Carnt tell a Norman from a gnome.	11/100
MATHS	: MENTAL -3/50 PROBLEMS -3/50.	TOTAL 6/100
GEOGRAPHY	: Thinks Greece is what you fry chips in	16/100
SCIENCE	: Made anti-freeze by putting her in fridge	19/100
P.E.	: Keeps tripping over his beard.	
TOTAL	:	Not a lot

POSITION IN CLASS: 46
TEACHER'S SIGNATURE: Miss Taycon.
HEADTEACHER: Should go far. The further the better.

I Canem

"Ah, yes . . ." she smiled, "I remember the boy now!" And Miss Taycon told us of some of Santa's problems in lessons.

"But he was good at poetry, the report said," I reminded her.

"Ah, yes! Wonderful poems he could write!"

Santa's old teacher smiled at the memory of her second-worst pupil.

"I wonder whatever became of him?" she asked.

"He became Father Christmas," I told her.

Miss Taycon nodded briskly. "Ah! I knew he had *something* to do with chimneys. Of course he was very kind and very popular! Now I come to think of it he wrote me a poem when he left the school . . . a sort of 'thank-you' poem. I still have it on the wall."

She pointed to a framed sheet of paper that hung on her wall. I read the moving poem . . .

175

To my Favourite Teecher - Miss Taycon.

My Teecher you're kind and you're cuddly,
  aT teeching us kids you're a winner.
I like you much more than my pet pussy-cat
And I like you much more than school dinner!

My teecher you're ever so clever
  You teeches us how to rite poems.
You teeches us two and two makes three or four
  And how Haly's a big town in Rome

My teecher knows all about naycher,
  How plants grow and why the bees buzz.
You never gets mad even when we are bad,
  Oh, how does you put up with uzz?

I'll miss the old school now I'm leaving.
  My poor little heart it is breakin'.
I'll miss all me friends but my love now I sends
  'Cos mostly I'll miss you Miss Taycon.

The teacher wiped a tear from the corner of her
eye and sniffled into a handkerchief.

Sherlock opened his mouth to ask a question, but I jumped in first.

"And can you remember what sort of pupil !Burp! Pardon was?"

"What do you want to know about him for?" Sherlock sighed. "He has nothing to do with our case."

"I'm not so sure, Sherl," I told him. "A boy who could write a poem like that could never grow up to be a thief!" I turned back to the teacher. "Do you remember !Burp!?" I asked.

"Ah, yes. If Santa was second-worst in 1T then young Pardon was the very worst. At least Santa was a kind, gentle boy. But !Burp! was wicked! Did you know he used to pull the legs off dolls?"

"We have heard," I said. "Was he as stupid in class?"

"Not stupid!" she snapped. "Awkward!"

The teacher shook her head. "And !Burp! was always late. I once asked him why. He said it was because there were eight in his family – and the alarm was only set for seven! Another time he said he was late because his father ran over himself that morning. Of course I was very concerned so I called to see !Burp!'s dad and he explained. His dad had asked !Burp! to run over to the shops for a loaf of bread. !Burp! refused . . . so his dad had run over himself!"

Sherlock sighed. "Very interesting, I'm sure, but not very important."

"Sorry, Sherl," I muttered.

"Don't call me Sherl," Sherl said.

"Sorry, Sherl . . . er, Sherley."

"And don't call me Shirley!" he moaned, steam coming out of his pipe.

"Sorry, Sherl . . . ock!" I smiled.

He turned to the old teacher and asked, "What we really want to know is what happened to Santa Claus when he left school?"

Miss Taycon drew a deep breath through her channel-tunnel nostrils. "He became a right little tearaway!"

"No!" I gasped. "Surely!"

"Don't call me Shirley!" Sherlock screamed.

"No! No! No!" I said quickly before he pushed

his magnifying glass into my big mouth –
sideways! "I meant *surely* Santa didn't turn bad!"

Miss Taycon shrugged her large shoulders.
"Got in with a bad crowd – with that !Burp!
Pardon's gang!"

"A gang! What did they do?" I asked.

"They dressed in leather clothes . . ."

"They bought some two-stroke, twin-cylinder
sleighs . . ."

"They fitted supercharged reindeer . . ."

"And they raced them round and round the
North Pole!"

"No one was safe on the roads!"

(!!Important Footnote!! Penguins do *not* live at the North Pole – they live at the South Pole. But you sometimes get a lost penguin wandering around and kindly nuns take them home! OK? That's sorted that out. Now we can get on with the story.)

"No one could sleep at night for the jingle and the clangle of the harnesses."

"Their name struck terror into the heart of every polar bear north of the Sahara desert!"

"They were . . ."

I asked Santa's old teacher how his days as a Bell's Angel ended. Seems he had a nasty accident once.

Santa escaped with just a bruised beard . . . but the reindeer was a write-off.

Miss Taycon told us how sorry Santa was about the crash. He never forgot how to drive a speeding sleigh – and that came in useful later! But he has always been kind to his reindeer ever since.

What I wanted to know was, what happened to !Burp! Pardon. But Sherlock asked, "What did Santa do after his crash?"

"Luckily he found himself a nice girlfriend and settled down . . . she lives just a few doors down. Why not pop along and see her?"

We had just nine hours left to save Christmas
. . . but Santa's girlfriend might be able to give us
a clue. We had to go.

"Her name is Helen . . . Nellie for short!"

We dashed to the door.

"But, Sherl!" I cried. "We don't know where
she lives!"

But the great detective hurried down the street
and into a cottage with "H" on the door.

"Helen-entry, my dear Sherlock," I muttered,
"I should have known!"

A cheerful old lady answered the door and
grinned. Her cheeks were as rosy as a tomato and
her teeth as yellow as best butter. Her white hair
was pulled back in a bun – it was a bread bun and
the crumbs were falling down her back.

"Here! I know you!" she cried.

Sherlock blushed.

"You're that famous detective! I've seen you
on the telly!"

"Well, madam . . ." Sherlock began.

"I think you're brilliant! Eeeh! Wait till I tell
my friends . . . I've met Agatha Christie."

Sherlock sniffed. "Actually, I'm *not* Agatha
Christie – I'm the famous Sherlock Gnomes –
I'm on the trail of the even famouser Santa Claus.
I wondered if you could answer some questions!"

"Come in, come in!" she smiled and led the way into her small cosy cottage. On the mantelpiece stood a picture of Santa himself.

"You were a friend of his?" I asked.

She sighed. "My very first boyfriend! Every time he saw me in the street he used to run and hide!"

"He did?" Sherlock asked.

"Well . . . he was very shy as a young man," she explained.

"But at last I sent my pet dog out to catch him and bring him back. A cute little hound called Buttercup!"

DON'T WORRY THE DOG'S A VEGETARIAN. HE ONLY EATS GREENGROCERS!

She explained that all she wanted was one of Santa's famous poems.

"And he wrote one for you?" I asked.

"Eventually," she cooed. "After I'd locked him in the garden shed for two days without any food! Ahh! He was so shy!"

"Hmm!" Sherlock muttered. "Have you still got this poem?"

She took it lovingly from a drawer and spread it on the table in front of us. It wasn't one of Santa's best – and the handwriting was very shaky.

"He must have been *very* shy when he wrote this. Nervous even!"

Nellie nodded. "Probably because Buttercup was smiling at him!"

I read the poem . . .

LOVE POME TO NELLIE.

I know a young lady, her name it is Nellie,
And each time I see her me knees turn to jelly.
It could be her smile, or her nose red and wet...
Or it could be the dirty great teeth of her pet!

I know a young lady, a wonderful sight,
Her teeth are like stars – 'cos they come out at night
Her love is as great as the princess and frog...
So I'll hop it when I get away from this dog.

I know a young lady she's fat and she's fair
And my heart strings are tied – like my legs to this chair.
I'll never leave Nellie, her slave I'll become...
At least till her doggie lets go of me bum!

Santa Claus.

"Er . . . very moving," I said.

"Yes," Nellie sniffed. "So sad. So sad. He's dead, you know!"

Sherlock jumped to his feet. "Impossible! Santa can't be dead!"

Nellie looked at him blankly. "Not Santa . . . Buttercup, stupid."

"Oh!"

"He ate someone that didn't agree with him," she sighed. Then she looked up brightly. "Would you like to meet my new dog?" she asked.

I beat Sherlock to the door by a centimetre. "No thanks!" I said quickly. "Just tell us what happened to Santa!"

188

"Oh, he got a job," she shrugged. "I remember seeing it advertised in the *North Pole Times* . . . everyone said he should apply for it. They said he was a natural, what with the whiskers and all that!"

"What sort of job was it?" Sherlock asked.

Nellie took another scrap of paper from the drawer and pushed it across the table to us.

WANTED!
A white-bearded person to do the job of Father Christmas!
Must be a good sleigh driver
51 Weeks' holiday a year
Free uniform – provide your own reindeer.
No pay but lots of gnomes to help
Single people only need apply
Apply to. Old Father Christmas
Ice Palace, The North Pole.

WANTED!

"Of course Santa applied. He knew it meant we could never be married – but he made that great sacrifice because he loves helping people!" Nellie explained.

"So, Old Father Christmas was retiring, was he?" I asked.

Nellie nodded. "He only does quiet jobs now – like sitting in shops in December and dishing out presents to children. He's too old to do all that flying around!"

"So, Old Father Christmas gave the job to the thieving Santa Claus, eh?" Sherlock guessed.

"I'm not sure," I began.

"Santa wasn't very bright," Nellie admitted, "but he was never a thief."

"He is now!" Sherlock snapped. "Docker Watson here saw him with his own two ears, didn't you, Doc?"

"Well, I . . ."

"Let's go and see the Old Father Christmas. See what made him trust a toy nicker. Always thought he was Saint Nickerless!" Gnomes went on, sucking his pipe.

"He still lives in the Ice Palace," Nellie told us. She told us a lot more. She told us so much that we thought we'd never get away. At last the desperate detective leapt to his feet.

"Let's go, my dear Watson!" Sherlock cried.

190

"We've only got seven hours left to save this Christmas."

"Cup of tea before you go?" Nellie asked.

"Please!" I said.

"Lemon?"

"No, thanks, I never eat raw lemons! Yeuch!" I told her.

"No! No! No!" Sherlock groaned. "Not tea *and* a lemon . . . lemon-*in*-tea, my dear Watson!"

And so we made our way to the palace of Old Father Christmas.

It was a fabulous palace made entirely of ice! The tourists loved it! – but the sparrows weren't so keen. Every time they landed on the roof they slid off!

And it was an absolute nightmare for window-cleaners!

191

We stood at the mighty Ice Gate to the palace and
wondered how to get in.

"Tap on the door, Watson!"

"Can't do that, Sherlock."

"Why not?"

"Because we did that joke on page 152!"

"Then jingle his bells!"

193

The door was answered by a maid on ice-skates.

"Is Old Father Christmas at home?" Sherlock asked.

"Eh?" the maid asked, cupping a hand to her deaf ear. Unfortunately the cup was full of hot tea.

"He said is Old Father Christmas at home?" I shouted.

"A gnome?" she said. "No! Old Father Christmas isn't a gnome – but he has some gnomes working for him."

The old maid passed us each a pair of ice skates and said, "Follow me!"

Sherlock pulled the skates on and sighed, "I like to slip into something comfortable now and then!" Just as he said it he slipped into an icy wall! Ouch! Great detective – awful skater.

The maid showed us through the icy palace till at last we came to a comfortable sitting room. She offered to announce us.

"Who shall I say is calling?" she asked.

"I'm Docker Watson . . ."

"There's a doctor to see you, Old Father Christmas!" she yelled at the old man in the red, fur-trimmed coat.

"Ah good! Doctor! Doctor! My kidneys are bad. What should I do?"

"Take them back to the butcher," Sherlock suggested. "Now breathe out sharply three times."

"You want to check my lungs?" the old man asked.

"No! I want to clean my magnifying glass," the great detective told him.

"But I can't keep food down. Everything I swallow keeps coming up!" Old Father Christmas complained.

"Then quick! Swallow my football pools!" Sherlock cried.

It took us a long time, but at last we convinced him that we weren't doctors and got down to the point of our visit.

"We're trying to find out the truth about Santa Claus – he's been pinching presents," Sherlock explained.

"Oh, dear!" the old man exclaimed. "Doesn't sound like him at all!"

"Docker Watson here saw it all!" Sherlock said sadly.

"I thought you said he wasn't a doctor! I have this problem with my red suit . . ."

"Don't start that again," I groaned.

"I keep wanting to wear a gold suit instead!" the old man said.

"Just a gilt complex," Sherlock snapped. "Now tell us how you came to employ this villain Claus!"

"Well, it all started when I decided to retire, a hundred years ago – we Father Christmases live a very long time, you know. To tell the truth I was getting too old and fat to get down the chimneys."

"Don't tell me," I muttered, "it didn't soot you any more?"

He ignored me. I don't really blame him.

He went on, "I put an advert in the *North Pole Times*. Only two people applied."

"Santa Claus was one," Sherlock said smugly.

"How did you know?" Old Father Christmas gasped.

"I'm a detective," Sherlock shrugged, "I guessed."

"And the other one was . . ."

"!Burp! Pardon," I put in quickly.

"Amazing!" the old man said. "Are you a detective too?"

"No. I'm a docker!"

"Then, doctor, maybe you can tell me why I feel so dog tired!"

"How long have you felt like this?"

"Ever since I was a puppy!"

"But tell us about the interviews," Sherlock cut in.

"Ah, yes. The interviews. I interviewed !Burp! Pardon first . . . I asked him if he liked children."

Old Father Christmas thought it was a bit odd that he said his favourite toys were dolls.

"I remember, he didn't own a reindeer, which could have been a problem. Seems he had had one but it crashed and broke an antler."

OLD FATHER CHRISTMAS:	You'd need a reindeer for this job.
!BURP!:	That's alright, I'd hire one.

"I was tempted to give him the job . . . but he wasn't as pleasant as young Santa Claus . . . and I thought his dark glasses might scare the kids," Old Father Christmas explained.

"The thief that I saw was wearing dark glasses!" I told Sherlock.

"Aha! A clever plot by Santa Claus to put the blame on !Burp! Pardon, see?"

"Er . . . no! I don't see," I muttered.

"So how did you come to hire this Santa character?" Sherlock asked.

"He seemed so keen to do the job he dashed straight out and bought a second-hand reindeer . . ."

"Santa explained that he knew nothing about reindeer and honest Arfur said he had just the animal he needed. That was the first time Santa Claus set eyes on his famous friend, Rudolph!"

Of course Santa was hopeless at sums, Old Father
Christmas explained, but he did notice that the
reindeer had a very red, shining nose.

THERE'S SOMETHING WRONG WITH
ITS NOSE!

BUT WHAT HAPPENED
TO IT?

LITTLE ACCIDENT SIR. SOON HAVE
IT RE-SPRAYED BLACK FOR YOU-OR
YELLOW'S VERY FASHIONABLE
THIS YEAR.

GLAD YOU ASKED ME THAT SIR...
NOW NOT A LOT OF PEOPLE
KNOW THIS...

And Arfur Chance went on to describe how
Rudolph came to get his red nose . . . .

Arfur explained that Rudolph was a very
famous reindeer. One day his owner had been
taking a short-cut across a frozen pond when the
ice cracked and the sleigh slipped in.

Rudolph tore himself free and galloped off for
help as the sleigh was slowly sinking. He couldn't

use the phone to call help so, instead, he galloped up to the top of the church tower and rang the bell – an alarm bell.

The fire brigade rushed out and saved the sleigh . . . but Rudolph was left with a badly battered conk.

So Santa bought Rudolph the red-nosed reindeer . . . but couldn't afford to have his nose resprayed. Old Father Christmas told us that it's been that way ever since.

"But, Sherlock!" I said excitedly. "The reindeer on my roof – the one that flew off with my presents! It had a *black* nose!"

"So?"

"So . . . it wasn't Rudolph!" I cried.

But Sherlock had the answer to that. "Everyone knows that great criminals use stolen cars for bank robberies. Santa must have used a stolen reindeer for a toy robbery!"

"I suppose so," I agreed glumly. After all – Sherlock was the world's greatest living detective. Still, I couldn't believe that the great poet and popular young Santa could have grown up to be a thief.

"And Santa Claus took over from you?" the detective went on.

Old Father Christmas nodded. "Had to train him first, of course . . ."

But Old Father Christmas wasn't going to give up that easily . . .

Old Father Christmas chuckled as he remembered that trick. But then he sighed and said, "Maybe that's what went wrong. Maybe after a hundred years of getting it right he's getting it backwards."

"I see!" Sherlock said. "*Taking* the toys instead of *giving* them! Elementary, my dear Watson."

But I shook my head. "Then why didn't he take *all* of the toys? How come he only took the dolls?"

"Ah! Oh!" Sherlock spluttered. "You didn't tell me that!" he objected.

"I thought I did. Maybe I forgot," I mumbled.

He pointed his magnifying glass at me and said, "You'll never make a great detective. First you suspect the innocent !Burp! Pardon – and then you forget things!"

"Sorry, Sherlock . . . where to next?"

"Er . . . I've forgotten!"

Old Father Christmas said, "If I were you I'd pop down to the gnomes' toy workshop. They'll be all ready to load up in time for Santa leaving . . . three hours from now. If they don't know what's become of him then no one will!" That didn't leave us much time! We had to get going again immediately!

Sherlock jumped to his feet. "Just what I was going to suggest. We'll interview the gnomes and chat to the reindeer!"

"Oh, Sherlock!" I laughed. "You can't chat to the reindeer! You're talking through your hat!"

"Of course I am!" he grinned. "It's a deerstalker hat!"

There was no answer to that.

The kind old man offered us food before we went. "Have a cake!" he offered.

"Thanks!" I smiled.

Old Father Christmas rang a bell. "The cakes were baked by my maid."

"Wonderful!" Sherlock cried. "I *love* gnome-maid cakes!"

So, full of tea and cherry cake, we set off down Reindeer Road to the Father Christmas workshops. But time was short – nearly as short as Sherlock – and it was growing dark!

Father Christmas's workshops were set in a huge log building. There were a dozen doors or more and outside each one stood a sleigh, loaded with sacks. Not a gnome was in sight.

"Which door shall we try?" I wondered. Each entry had letters above it. "A/B Entry", "C/D Entry" and so on.

"Different entries for different countries," Gnomes explained.

"Don't tell me!" I said suddenly. "Let me guess!" And I headed for the door with L/M above it.

Sherlock nodded, but before he could say anything I beat him to it. "L/M Entry, my dear Sherlock!"

"Correct!"

I knocked. From behind the door came a frightened voice.

"Who's there?"

"Docker!"

"Doctor Who?"

"No. Not Doctor Who, I'm Docker Watson!"

"You can't come in!"

"Why not?"

"Because you may be the great toy robber!"

Sherlock stepped forward. "I am the famous Sherlock Gnomes. I can solve anything!"

There was a muttering behind the door then another voice said, "Then solve this riddle . . . What is green, made of concrete and grows in fields?"

The gnomes let us in and dragged the great detective to a stool by a roaring log fire. Each one had his or her name on the front of their green overall.

"You have to help us!" Gnorman groaned. "Two hours to Christmas Day and Father Christmas is missing!"

"I can't help you!" Sherlock gasped. "I'm too old to climb down chimneys!"

"Santa Claus is older than you!" Gnora the Gnome pointed out.

"Ah!" Sherlock said. "But he's had stacks of practice!"

"We don't want you to take his place," Gnigel the Gnome said. "We want you to find him! Otherwise we'll have to give all the dolls away to the kidnapper!"

"Kidnapper!" Sherlock scoffed. "What makes you think he's been kidnapped?"

"We've had a note," Gnora the Gnome said, and she pushed it into Sherlock's hand.

Dear Gnomes and Dear Deer,
I have your Father Christmas. He is My prisoner. Bring me all the dolls in your factory by midnight on Christmas eve or Christmas is cancelled this year! I will be waiting in the house of that kind old man! Burp! Pardon.
You have been warned!
Ron Buppard

"See, Sherlock!" I cried. "Ron Buppard! Rearrange the letters of Ron Buppard and what do you get?"

"Er . . . Barr Up Pond?" he suggested.

"No! It's !Burp! Pardon!"

"But !Burp! Pardon can't be the Great Toy Robber," he objected.

"Why not?"

"Because he's a kind old man . . . it says so in the letter!"

Which just goes to show. Even the world's greatest detective can be pretty thick sometimes!

I dashed to the door. "Follow me!" I called to Sherlock and the gnomes.

I jumped on the sleigh with the red-nosed reindeer hitched up while the others piled on the sledge pulled by a cross-eyed reindeer.

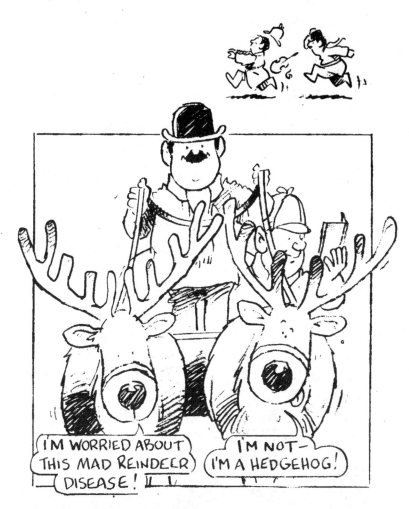

It was a long drive to !Burp! Pardon's house and Sherlock became bored. So he rummaged in one of the toy sacks and came out with a book to read.

"What are you reading?" I asked.

"The tale of the princess and the frogs!"

"I thought it was just one frog . . . the princess kissed it and it turned into a prince!"

"No-o!" Sherlock said. "This is different. In the first story the princess kissed a stupid frog."

"What happened?"

"It turned into a tadpole!"

"What about the next story?"

"That's about the greedy princess. She married a rich old frog then just waited for him to croak!"

At last we reached a lonely cottage standing in a field of snow. Moonlight glinted on a loaded

sleigh, piled with sacks. And every sack was overflowing with dolls.

"We'll have to be careful!" Sherlock whispered as we pulled up by the lighted window. We peered over the sill into the little room. A fire blazed in the hearth, and there was Santa Claus – tied to a chair with a white-bearded man in dark glasses sitting in front of him. !Burp! Pardon. The one who pinched my presents!

"You see!" I hissed. "!Burp! Pardon *is* the villain! It's only half an hour to midnight. !Burp! pulls the arms off dolls. What will he do to Santa Claus?"

"You could be right, Watson!" Sherlock admitted.

"Santa Claus is just an 'armless old man," I moaned.

"He will be if we don't rescue him!" the Great Detective said grimly. "We need a plan!"

"Rush in and free him!" I suggested.

"Don't be stupid," Sherlock snapped.

"What do you suggest?" I asked.

Sherlock thought as precious minutes ticked away. "I think . . . we should rush in and free him!"

"Great idea!" I urged.

Sherlock slipped around the corner while I watched through the window.

Two minutes later the great detective returned.

Suddenly !Burp! Pardon's voice carried through the window. "Twenty minutes, Santa!"

Santa shook his sad old head. "Ah, !Burp! Why are you doing this?"

"So that no one in the world can have a doll for Christmas!"

"But why? Why? Why?"

"Because, when I was a little boy, no one ever let *me* have a doll for Christmas! They said that boys can't have dolls! So I tore the legs off all the girls' dolls – if I couldn't have one then they couldn't have them either! See!"

"That's mean," Santa said.

"I don't care. And soon I'll have all the dolls in the whole wide world! That'll fettle them!" !Burp! cried.

"But if you don't set me free then *no one* will get a present for Christmas this year!" Santa pleaded.

"And why should they?" !Burp! sniffed.

"Because we always give presents at Christmas," Santa said gently.

"Since when?"

"Since nearly two thousand years ago . . . haven't you ever heard the story of the first Christmas?" Santa asked. When !Burp! shook his head Santa went on, "I once wrote a poem about it. Do you want to hear it?"

!Burp! nodded. "You always did write great poems, Santa!" he said, and unfastened the ropes that held his old school mate.

Santa rubbed his wrists. Sherlock, the gnomes and the reindeer and I all gathered around the window to listen as Santa recited his story . . .

THE FIRST CHRISTMAS

The shepherds were watching their flock in the fields
While stars in the dark sky were flitting.
Thomas was carving a fine wooden doll . . .
While young Jim got on with his knitting
. . . a scarf.

As Tommy remarked, "That's a big star up there!"
An angel came down with a bound.
Old Tom dropped the doll and young Jim dropped a stitch . . .
While the sheep ran around and around
. . . in circles.

The angel just folded his wings and he grinned,
"Halo, lads! Get along to the tavern!
A baby is born, it's the child of the Lord!
Take some prezzies and let the babe have 'em . . .
please."

"We cannot do that! You great feathered fool!"
Old Tom stood and started to shout.
"The sheep'll get got by the greedy old wolf!"
But the angel said, "I'll sort him out! . . . don't
worry."

But still the old man he was fussing about.
"I haven't got no gifts at all!"
But Jim said, "I'll take the young baby me scarf,
And you, Tom, can give it the doll. . . if you like."

The Angel said, "That's very kind of you lads,
But don't forget Joseph and Mary."
So Jim said, "We'll take them a nice little lamb –
That one there is all cuddly and hairy
. . . and fat."

The shepherds went trotting down Bethlehem
Hill
And they followed the star where it shines.
"Look at that!" Tommy cried, "There's three
camels down there!
And they've parked them on two yellow lines
. . . they'll be for it!"

Now the shepherds felt shy as they crept in the
back
Of the stable and saw who it were!
Three great kings standing there with their arms
full of gifts,
Stuff like gold, frankincense and some myrrh
. . . very posh!

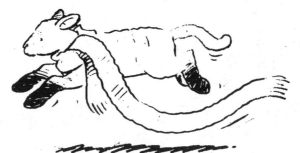

Jim's small lamb it went "Baa!", mother Mary said, "Ahh!

Come on in! Put your gifts by the bed."
Tommy said, "Sorry, lady, our gifts aren't so grand

As them blokes with the towels round their heads!"

... he meant turbans.

Mary loved Jimmy's scarf, it would keep the child warm,

And the lamb's wool could make her a frock!
"In fact, Joseph," she said to her husband that night,

"We could even start up our own flock
... think of that!"

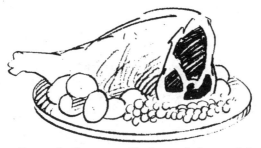

(Now Joseph just smiled and he said, "Very
nice,"
But the truth was his smile was a sham.
To be honest he'd looked at the gift and he'd
thought,
"Tasty chops – or a nice leg of lamb!
. . . yum, yum, yum!")

Poor old Tommy felt sick as a six-year-old chip,
As he held out his wood doll so sad.
"Sorry, lady," he groaned, "but the chap with the
wings,

Never mentioned the babe was a lad
. . . he won't want dolls!"

Mary smiled very kind at the shepherd so old
And the wood doll was really quite beautiful.
"It's the thought, not the gift, that's what
matters," she said.
"And who knows, but it might come in useful!"
. . . she was right.

Meanwhile, back in the palace, bad King Herod
had heard
Of a new king and he was real cross.
So he sent out his men for to find him and snatch
him,
And make jolly sure he got lost
. . . for good!

When the shepherds returned to their sheep in
the hills,

Leaving Mary and Joseph in danger,
Twenty soldiers burst in to the stable that night
And they snatched up the babe from the manger
. . . that was that!

But Joseph just laughed and his wife Mary smiled
As she slipped the babe from her cloak's creases.
And the soldiers so dim never knew to this day . . .
'Twas the wood doll that they'd chopped to pieces
. . . served them right!

So when Christmas time comes we remember the
first gifts
From good kings and shepherds in tatters.
And the words of the lady so wise when she said,
"It's the thought, not the gift, that's what
matters."
. . . Merry Christmas!

And Santa Claus finished his poem as the clock creaked around to midnight. The only sound was the soft sniffle of !Burp! Pardon.

"What did you say happened to the doll? Chopped to pieces!" he sighed.

"Turned out to be a valuable gift after all – even for a boy, didn't it?" Santa Claus smiled.

"Poor doll," the gnome in the dark glasses groaned.

"I thought you hated dolls – pulled their legs off," Santa argued.

"Only out of spite – only 'cos no one let me have one," !Burp! muttered miserably. "I hate to think that I'm as rotten as that nasty Herod! Poor doll!"

"Ho! No!" Santa said cheerily. "There'll always be plenty of dolls . . ." then the smile slid from his face, "except this year, of course."

Midnight started to strike.

!Burp! Pardon looked at Santa guiltily. "It's Christmas morning! The children will be waking up in a couple of hours . . . and finding their stockings empty!" he murmured.

Santa nodded sadly. "Even if I set off now I'd be struggling to make it before morning. Not without some help!"

"I'll help!" !Burp! cried. "My sleigh is outside . . . and I'm faster than you!"

As they hurried out into the snowy night Sherlock and I slid back into the shadows.

"Look!" Santa cried. "Here's my Rudolph! And all of my gnomes! With your help, !Burp!, we might just make it!"

Santa and !Burp! jumped aboard their sleighs. With a cry of "Hi-ho, Rudolph, away!" and a jingling of bells they rode off into the night.

WHO IS THAT MAN?

THAT, SON, IS !BURP! PARDON.

GRANTED... BUT YOU'LL HAVE TO STOP DRINKING SO MUCH POP!

So Sherlock Gnomes had saved Christmas for the children – with a little help from me, Docker Watson, and a lot of help from Santa's Christmas poem. The trouble was we were stuck at the North Pole.

KNOCK! KNOCK! WATSON

WHO'S THERE SHERLOCK?

WENCESLAS!

WENCESLAS WHO?

WENCESLAS TRAM BACK TO FELIXSTOWE?

I THINK WE'VE JUST MISSED IT!

I asked, "How do we get home, Gnomes?"

Even the great detective didn't have the answer to everything. "Walk, I suppose."

And we set off to walk back to Felixstowe. There was snow on the ground, snow in the sky

and snow as far as the eye could see. But, with the great Sherlock Gnomes for company, I was never bored.

"I spy with my little eye something beginning with 'S'." I said.

After just half an hour Sherlock had guessed it. "Snow!" he exclaimed.

"Amazing, my dear Gnomes," I gasped.

"Elementary, my dear Watson," he shrugged.

"But how did you guess?" I asked.

"Because I am the world's greatest detective," he smiled.

I shook my head in wonder at the great man's talent. "My turn," he said as we came to the edge of a forest full of Christmas trees. "I spy with my little eye something beginning with 'S'."

"Er . . . snow?"

"No."

"Er . . . Sherlock?"

"No."

"Er . . . six-ton sausage roll?"

"There isn't one," Sherlock pointed out.

"No – but if there was I'd eat it all," I groaned. "Alright, Sherlock, I give up. What do you spy with your little eye beginning with 'S'?"

He pointed at a fir tree. "Shrub!"

And the world's greatest detective and I went home for a cup of tea . . . sitting by a Christmas tree loaded with presents for the kids.

Santa had made it after all.

235

So now you know how Christmas almost ended
with no toys,
How the children nearly woke up to disaster.
But thanks to Father Christmas and his gnomes
(and Rudolph too)
He whizzed around the world just that bit faster.

Remember, then, that Christmas time's not fun
for everyone.
So don't just think of getting – think of giving.
If people cruel or jealous try to make your life too
hard,
Then you should try forgetting – and forgiving.

236